Satan's War on ~~Free~~ Agency

Greg Wright

Copyright © 2003 by Greg Wright
All Rights Reserved

No part of this book may be reproduced in any form whatsoever, whether by graphic, visual, electronic, filming, microfilming, tape recording, or any other means, without the prior written permission of the authors, except in the case of brief passages embodied in critical reviews and articles where the title, authors and ISBN accompany such review or article.

This book is not an official publication of The Church of Jesus Christ of Latter-day Saints. All opinions expressed herein are the author's alone and are not necessarily those of the distributor or of The Church of Jesus Christ of Latter-day Saints.

Distributed by:

Granite Publishing and Distribution, LLC
868 North 1430 West
Orem, Utah 84057
(801) 229-9023 • Toll Free (800) 574-5779
Fax (801) 229-1924

Page Layout & Design by Myrna Varga, The Office Connection, Inc.
Cover Design by Steve Gray

Library of Congress Control Number: 2002117651
ISBN: 1-930980-06-Y

First Printing, July 2003
Second Printing, February 2004

Printed in the United States of America

10 9 8 7 6 5 4 3 2

Table of Contents

Introduction	....	vii
Preface:	THE POWER OF A QUESTION	xi
Chapter 1:	THE AGENCY FORMULA	1
Chapter 2:	WHAT IS CHOICE?	5
	Choice Is Simply Having Options	5
	Choice Is Having the Power to Choose	6
	"I Don't Have a Choice"	7
Chapter 3:	WHAT IS FREEDOM?	9
	There Is No Freedom Without Law	9
	There Is No Freedom Without Cost	10
	There Is No Freedom Without Penalty	11
	Alternative Definitions of Freedom	13
	Political Freedom: Choice Without Penalty	13
	Political Freedom Contrasted with Spiritual Freedom	14
	Spiritual Freedom: Choice Without Compulsion	16
	Act for Yourselves	17
	Three Elements of Spiritual Freedom	18
	Freedom Through the Atonement	19
	Free to Choose Means Free to Lose	21
Chapter 4:	WHAT IS AGENCY?	23
	The Importance of Understanding Agency	23
	Agency = Stewardship	25
	Dictionary Definitions of Agency	25
	Stewards in Ancient Scripture	27
	Stewards and Agents in Modern Scripture	27
	The Lord's Definition of Agency	29
	Agency = Accountability	29
	Freedom + Knowledge = Agency = Accountability .	30
	The Three Elements of Agency	33
	Free Agency Isn't Free	34
	The Damning Doctrine of Unaccountability	35

Chapter 5:	FROM LUCIFER TO PERDITION	39
	Lucifer the Morning Star	39
	Lucifer Wanted to Be the Messiah	41
	When the Messiah Was Chosen	41
	Lucifer's Lust for Power	44
	Lucifer's Campaign Begins	45
Chapter 6:	THE APPEAL OF SATAN'S PLAN	47
	An Error Corrected	47
	How Did We Get the "Force" Idea?	48
	A Rebellion of Compulsion or Persuasion?	49
	What Motivated the Rebellion?	50
	The Story of the Three Universities	52
	Force College	
	University of Freedom	
	Law School	
	Which School Represents Which Plan?	53
	What Do the Scriptures Say?	55
	The University of Freedom Is Satan's Plan	60
Chapter 7:	SATAN'S FORCE PLAN	61
	The Force Plan Is Not Scriptural	61
	The Force Plan Is Not Logical	62
	The Force Plan Is Not Appealing	64
	A Brilliant Masterpiece of Deception	66
Chapter 8:	SATAN'S FREEDOM PLAN	67
	The False Freedom of Saving Men in Sin	68
	The Freedom Plan Limits Results Not Choices	69
	Satan—the Accuser and the Salesman	70
	The Consequences of Having No Consequences	72
	Religious and Secular Popularity of the Freedom Plan	73
	Grace and Accountability	75
	The Freedom Plan Was an Attempt to Destroy Accountability	76
Chapter 9:	THE GADIANTONS USED THE FREEDOM PLAN	79
	The Incredible Success of the Gadiantons	79
	What Is a "Secret Combination"?	81

    Corrupt People are the Key to Success 81
    The Source of Gadianton Doctrine 83
    Corrupting The Legal System 83
    "Fair Promises" Bring Protection and Election 84
    The Surrender to Seduction 86
    The Symbiotic Relationship Turned Parasitic 88

Chapter 10: MODERN GADIANTONS 91
    A Hand Up or a Hand Out? 92
    Dependence Is Not Independence 94
    Hollywood Gadiantons 95
    Flattering People with a New Vocabulary 95
    Some "Politically Correct" Examples 97
    The War in Heaven Brought to Earth 98

Chapter 11: SATAN'S WAR ON THE FAMILY 101
    The Perfect Parent 101
    Applying God's Principles Appropriately 102
    The Main Problem 103
    Love Without Law 104
    When There's Law at Home 106
    How to Raise an Irresponsible Child 109
    How to Raise a Responsible Child 112

Chapter 12: "WAR" STORIES 117
    The Murphys 118
    The Old Couch 121
    Are You Happy? 123
    A Chat with Mr. Freedom 125
    A Chat with Mr. Law 127
    The Lost Sheep, Coin and Son 128
    The Solder Gun 131
    A Cheek for a Cheek 133
    Tonya in the Nursery 136
    In Conclusion 139

Scriptural Index 143

Index 147

today, or is it the same as it was during the War in Heaven?

To underestimate Satan is a big mistake. To casually assume that we know enough about him can result in a very painful surprise. When we comprehend the true principles of agency, we can identify the clever lies in Satan's philosophy. Deception can be dispelled by an understanding of agency, just as darkness is dispelled by light.

Preface

The Power of a Question

The right question can be the beginning of a journey to new knowledge and enlightenment. So it was for me on a Sunday afternoon after sacrament meeting in southern England many years ago. An enthusiastic young girl went in search of a missionary to answer her question. She was desperately trying to find a scripture to support a doctrine that she and a friend had been discussing. All she wanted was a scripture reference, so any elder would do.

There were other elders around, but as fate would have it, she found me. I was standing near the front door saying good-bye to members, watching for nonmembers and hoping for referrals when she approached me. Looking at my name badge, she said, "Elder Wright! You'll do," in that tart British accent that I was still trying to get used to. "I need you to find the scripture that says Satan's plan was to force us to be righteous so we could all go to heaven."

"No problem," I thought to myself as I opened my well-worn scriptures. I had been intensively studying the scriptures since I was fifteen and even had a reputation for being somewhat of a scriptorian. I knew there were several places in the scriptures that talked about the War in Heaven. I was confident that I could find the one she was looking for.

I turned to the first scripture I could find, and read it. That wasn't the one. Neither was the next or the next. After reading all the "War in Heaven" scriptures I knew of, I still had no answer for her. I told the young girl I would look it up during the week and give her the reference next Sunday. I was sure I would find it as in my apartment I had a full set of concordances for all four standard works that I had carried with me from the U.S.

That week I did my homework. I looked up every reference to Satan, the War in Heaven, force, plan, and anything else I could think of to find that scripture. My very best efforts, however, were not good enough. The next Sunday I told the young lady about my failure. My inability to find a scripture about Satan's plan to force us to be righteous confused me. I had plainly heard this doctrine when the missionaries first taught me the gospel at age thirteen. I had heard it many times since, both in Church meetings and seminary classes, and I had never questioned it. I had had no reason to, until now.

After that day, many questions about the War in Heaven began to plague me. I wasn't doubting the gospel. I knew *it* was true. I just wanted to understand it better. I wanted to know why an account of Satan's plan to force us to be righteous was not found in the scriptures. I wondered if it was doctrine or merely a well-established tradition.

Since then, I have run into other traditions that have turned out to be false. For instance, the idea that there will be so few sons of perdition that you can count them on one hand. I believed this until I failed to find it in the scriptures. Another previously believed tradition is that two plans were proposed in the pre-earth life, first Satan's and then Jesus's. Not only is this illogical in terms of what we know about our Father in Heaven, but it is not found in the scriptures. If this were true, we would have to believe that God did not know the best way to save His children until Jesus came up with the right idea.

Was this issue with Satan's plan of force also a false tradition? If not, then why didn't the scriptures teach it? If the scriptures do not teach it, then how did this interpretation come to be so well accepted in the Church?

I had gained a great respect for the scriptures. My habit was to try to find scriptural references to support the doctrines I was taught. I actually used to sit in church looking up scriptures about topics mentioned by the speakers. My objective was to "be ready always to give an answer to every man that asketh you a reason of the hope that is in you" (1 Peter 3:15). It was not enough to *know* the answers; I wanted to be able to *show* the answers, chapter and verse. I wanted to be ready to teach from the scriptures.

Harold B. Lee's example made a great impression on me. At the end of our stay in the Salt Lake Mission Home in 1973, all the missionaries had the once-in-a-lifetime opportunity to have a meeting with the Prophet in the upper room of the Salt Lake Temple. After our temple endowment session, we were escorted to the upper room where we had one hour to ask President Lee *any* question our young hearts and minds could come up with. We were told we could ask anything about anything, even the most sacred ordinances of the temple.

What absolutely astounded me was that President Lee not only answered every question, but that he did so from the scriptures. Being a student of the scriptures myself, I watched to see if he could do it every time. He did. At the end of our session, he held up his scriptures and told us that all of the answers he had shared with us could be found within its pages. He strongly urged us to search the scriptures for answers to all of our questions. I know now, as President Lee certainly knew then, that not every truth is in the scriptures. Not everything he ever taught was supported with a scripture, but almost every principle he taught was.

So it is with this book. I cannot promise to support every single point with the scriptures. But to be fair, the scriptures are not the *only* source of truth. The search for truth includes studying things out "in our own mind" (D&C 9:8), "even by study and also by faith" (D&C 88:118). The Lord also told us to "reason together" that we "may understand" (D&C 50:10). Study, reason and logic are valid methods of seeking gospel knowledge but are only safe when staying within the parameters of the standard works. Not every detail about the War of Heaven is in the scriptures, but there is enough written about it to safely extrapolate from what is.

Having no answer to that young girl's question lead me to other answers, but then, always more questions. One thing I did know a week later was that the scriptures did not teach that Satan planned to force us to be righteous. That concept simply wasn't there and I had to know why. This began my thirty-year journey to new knowledge and a better understanding of agency.

In the twenty-three years I have been teaching seminary and institute, I have taught the principle of agency both to my children and my students. I have taught it "line upon line" (Isaiah 28:10) as I have learned it through reasoning from, and pondering over, the scriptures. I have learned through my lifetime study of agency, that it is not just another gospel topic. Every single decision we make, as well as every thought we think, is an exercise of our agency (Mosiah 4:30; Alma 12:14). Since our eternal status depends upon everything we think and do, it is safe to say that the principle of agency is central to the entire plan of salvation. For this reason, I cannot think of anything that can influence our lives and the lives of our students and children more than the principle of agency. Since this principle can have such a profound effect upon every waking moment of our lives, is it not to our advantage to understand it? Are not those who understand agency the most likely to make the best use of it?

Sketch by Jeremiah Moore

Chapter 1

The Agency Formula

I had always thought that choice, freedom, and agency were the same thing, but after many years of studying and teaching the scriptures I have come to realize they are three separate yet interrelated concepts. Freedom is more than choice, and agency is more than freedom. A person can make a choice and not really be free. A person can be free and still not have agency.

In my classes, I have found that using a simple object lesson demonstrates the relationship between choice, freedom, and agency. I ask my students to participate in a demonstration with me, the single rule being that they assume the only choices they have are the ones I specifically give them. When they have all agreed, I put a coin in my hand, close my fist, and hold it in front of me. I ask one student to pick a hand. Although he may be momentarily confused because I am holding out only one hand, the student will eventually pick the hand with the coin in it, because it is the only one offered. I congratulate him, give him the coin, and ask the class, "Did he have a choice?"

In the discussion that follows, someone will invariably point out that the student did have a choice. He could have chosen the offered hand or refused to choose at all. I remind the class of the condition that they have only the choices I give them, and "not choosing" was not one of those choices.

Inevitably, most students will then concede that with only one option—the single offered hand—the student did not have true choice. "So it takes a minimum of two options to make an actual choice?" I ask, and when they agree, I write on the board:

2 options = choice

Next, I hold out two hands, both fists closed around a penny and repeat the first element. "To have a choice, all you need is two options." "So now pick one," I say to a student. But before opening whatever hand she picks, I ask the class, "Does she have agency?"

Because we have not yet discussed the differences between choice and agency, most of the students say yes. I let them discuss this a little but make no comments at this point. I simply open the hand and show the class the penny, then close the hand and ask the student to choose again. Nearly every time she will choose the other hand. I show the penny in the other hand, then open both hands and ask them the most critical question of the entire exercise: "Now does she have agency?"

Some students say yes, but many say no. I respond to the second group by saying, "I gave her two options, so why do some of you say that she has no agency? What else could be missing?" Someone then usually asserts that you have to have opposition. "True enough," I reply. "But in a sense I did give her opposite choices. Right is the opposite of left, correct? Let's say that my right hand represents a good choice and my left hand represents a bad one. Do we have agency with these two opposite choices?"

Chapter 1 ~ THE AGENCY FORMULA

To those who say no, I respond: "Why not? I have clearly offered two different options. What else could we possibly need?" It usually takes the students several moments of looking at the two pennies before someone figures it out: "You need opposite results!" At this point I write this formula on the board:

2 options + different results = freedom

"Excellent," I tell them. "In 2 Nephi 2:11 we read that there must be opposition in *all* things, so we need not only opposite choices, but also opposite, or at least different, results. This is what gives us freedom, and both freedom and choice must exist before we can have agency." I hold out my hands again, but this time with a penny in only one of them. "Pick again," I tell them. "This time the penny represents heaven and the absence of a penny represents hell. So choose wisely."

I offer different students the choice until someone picks the hand with no penny, then I open the empty hand. "Too bad. You have to go to hell because you made the wrong choice." Then I ask the class, "Did this person have agency?"

There are always students who will say yes, but also those who will say no. "Why do you say no?" I ask the latter group. "What is wrong? I gave everyone two options with different results. What more do we need?" Again, the students eventually come up with the right answer: "*We need knowledge.*"

"Knowledge of the choices, or knowledge of the results?" I ask.

"Knowledge of the results," they tell me. So I write the following on the board by the other formulas:

2 options + different results + knowledge of the results = agency

"So it's important to know something about the results, or

consequences, of a decision before we make a choice," I say as I hold out my hands yet again, putting the penny in the right one. "Pick a hand, but remember that if you want heaven, choose the right. If you want hell, choose the left." This time the student chooses the right, and I congratulate her on getting to go to heaven. "Now class, did she have agency?" I ask. And by now they are sure she did, because we have satisfied the formula showing the three requirements of agency. Now let us explore the elements of this formula in greater detail.

Chapter 2

What Is Choice?

Note: The next three chapters are doctrinal and somewhat analytical—rich in principles, but not easy reading. They are also essential in laying the doctrinal foundation needed to understand Satan's war. After these three chapters the story continues. There we will learn about Satan's character, his fall and how he deceived so many in the war in heaven. The rest of the book will show applications of Satan's battle plan and how he still uses it to destroy government and families.

A choice is a willful act or decision. Making a choice means to pick one from multiple options. To have a choice, all we need is at least two options. If there are not at least two options, there can be no real choice. Every scriptural use of the word "choose" is based on a decision involving at least two options.

Choice Is Simply Having Options

To have a choice, the options do not have to be opposite or even different as the scriptures reveal. Goliath, for instance, told the armies of Israel to "choose you a man for you, and let him come down to me" (1 Samuel 17:8). There were many men in the army from which to choose. Each would have been a separate choice, a different choice, but it cannot be said that they were opposite choices. There are plenty of examples of this kind every day. Every stroke on a keyboard is a different choice, so is every step we take, but they are not opposites. The principle of opposition most often comes into play when applied to choices between right and wrong. It is not found as often in common choices throughout the day.

Choices do not have to be opposite, or even different, in order to be separate choices.

When grocery shopping we may think about which kind of cereal to buy, then which size box we want. At this point we are choosing between different options. Once we have decided on the kind and size however, we still have to choose exactly which box of cereal to take. They are basically identical, so it doesn't make any real difference which one we choose, any more than it makes any difference which penny from all the pennies in the change tray the cashier gives us.

This concept seems so simple it is almost trivial. So why make the point at all? Because it is important to distinguish between choice and freedom. Having choice and being *free* to choose are related concepts, but they are not identical. Ultimately, understanding these differences will help expose the subtle and devious plan of Lucifer to destroy the agency of man.

Choice Is Having the
Power to Choose

Choice—having at least two options—is the first requirement of agency. We could also say that the first requirement of agency is having the *power* to choose, for it is the same thing. For example, the laws of nature have not given us the *power* to fly away like a bird simply by waving our hands. Since we do not have the power to fly like a bird, we do not have the option or choice to do so. Having no power to choose another option leaves us with only one option and with no choice.

Think back to the object lesson with the two pennies. When I offered only one hand, the student did not have another option. Because his *options were limited* to one, he did not have the *power* to choose anything else. It can be said either way, but most people are used to thinking in terms of limited options. If a cashier needs to give one penny in change to a customer and only has one penny left, she could say to herself, "I do not have the power to choose any other penny but the one I have left." She could also say to herself, "I don't have any choice but to use the one penny I have left." Both statements are correct but the second is simpler and more likely to be the way we think in most cases of limited choices.

"I Don't Have a Choice"

The statement, "I don't have a choice," or words to that effect, are common in our culture, but such statements are rarely true. What we usually mean is that we do not like the consequences of any of the other options.

Suppose a man is trapped in a burning building. He is crying for help from a window on the third floor. There is no safe way down and the fire department will not make it in time to save him. If he stays in the building, he will die. If he jumps he may also die, but he may get lucky and escape with only broken bones. We might say that he has "no choice" but to jump. In reality, however, he does have a choice, because he has more than one option. He can either stay on the third floor, or he can jump. Neither option is desirable, but there *are* two options, so this man does have a choice. The other undeniable fact is that he *will* choose between those two options. The consequences of his options are definitely a factor in what he decides to do, but the consequences have nothing to do with the fact that he has two options.

Now suppose that a woman is in the same predicament, only she is trapped in a burning building on the thirtieth floor. She too has two options: to stay or to jump. Either choice will result in death; the only difference is in the method of dying. Again, this woman *will* make a choice.

So, most of the time when we say we do not have a choice, we really do because we have more than one option. In most cases where people think they lack choice, what they really lack is freedom. Remember:

2 options = choice, and 2 options + different results = freedom.

Chapter 3

What Is Freedom?

There Is No Freedom Without Law

The effort to learn what freedom *is* might best begin with learning what freedom is *not*, which can be a painful lesson.

Growing up in the sixties, I saw a lot of young people searching for themselves, rebelling against "the establishment," and seeking for something they called freedom. Many of them defined freedom as freedom from the constraint of laws. Invariably, they were proven wrong. These people failed to grasp the truth that freedom *requires* laws.

The term "freedom" is used in many ways throughout scripture. It can refer to a condition without oppression, without compulsion, or without penalty, but in no case does it ever refer to a condition without law. There is *no* such condition. God has made it very clear that we will always be subject to laws. "And will I appoint unto you, saith the Lord, except it be by law?" (D&C 132:11). And again, "All kingdoms have a law given; . . . there is no space in the which there is no kingdom; . . . *And unto every kingdom is given a law; and unto every* law there are certain bounds also and conditions" (D&C 88:36–38; emphasis added).

Since there is no place without laws on earth, in heaven, or even in hell, we would do well to learn to enjoy laws by making good use of them.

Some people perceive laws to be restrictive. However, laws do not restrict. They simply designate what is good and evil; what is permitted and not permitted; what is legal and illegal; what is possible and impossible. Laws attach consequences to decisions. Without laws different decisions could not result in different consequences, resulting in no freedom. If a man insists that some laws restrict him, then he must also admit that other laws enable him. All things that are invented or created are accomplished only because laws make them possible. All things are governed and accomplished by laws, whether physical, social, or spiritual. Freedom, therefore, cannot be a place or condition without law. The fact is laws do not limit freedom. Laws actually make possible the condition of freedom. It is law that makes us free: "I, the Lord God, make you *free*, therefore ye are *free* indeed; and the law also maketh you *free*" (D&C 98:8; emphasis added).

There Is No Freedom Without Cost

Let us consider what the word "free" means using two scriptures from the Book of Mormon:

> Hath he commanded any that they should not partake of his salvation? Behold I say unto you, Nay; but he hath given it *free* for all men; [2 Nephi 26:27; emphasis added]
>
> And the way is prepared from the fall of man, and salvation is *free*. [2 Nephi 2:4; emphasis added]

Chapter 3 ～ WHAT IS FREEDOM?

As a young convert I thought that "free" in these verses meant that salvation was "without cost." I now realize that although it cannot be purchased with money, salvation does have a cost. True, we cannot buy it with money, but it will cost us at least two things: our pride and our sins. For some, this can be *very* expensive.

There Is No Freedom Without Penalty

Understanding the meaning of the words "free" or "freedom" can be crucial. The problem is, the meaning of the word "free" has been intentionally corrupted over time. Satan has twisted many words into alternate meanings in order to deceive us, and the words "free" and "freedom" are no exception. The following is a classic example of the age-old conflict over the meaning of the word "free." Korihor, the anti-Christ, accused Alma of not allowing his people to be free. "Ye say that this people is a *free* people. Behold, I say they are in bondage" (Alma 30:24; emphasis added).

In other words, what Alma called a state of freedom, Korihor labeled as a state of bondage. Their opposite opinions stemmed from contrasting definitions of the word "free." Alma was the chief judge at the time. As such he was responsible for maintaining the peace. As a part of his duties he was obligated to enforce the laws of the land by pronouncing penalties upon those who broke the laws. "But if he murdered he was punished unto death; and if he robbed he was also punished; and if he stole he was also punished; and if he committed adultery he was also punished" (Alma 30:10–11).

Korihor was a very clever man. It is not likely that he objected to the enforcement of laws that preserved the civilization and privileges he enjoyed. How could he say that the people were in bondage when he knew very well that the Nephites enjoyed political freedom? The answer is that Korihor's criticism was not only political; but also religious. He criticized Alma, as chief judge, for teaching the people his religion, which Korihor called mere "tradition" (Alma 30:28). The problem with stopping Korihor was that "there was no law against a man's beliefs," meaning that people could only be punished for crimes. No one was punished for their beliefs. This included Korihor, and he knew it. How then could he accuse Alma of keeping the people in bondage?

Korihor was free to preach his doctrine all he liked. So he was not attacking the Nephite leaders for preserving those civil laws which gave him freedom to preach. Korihor understood that the enforcement of good laws was necessary to preserve civilization. However, Korihor *was* objecting to laws that he considered religious rather than civil.

He did not like one particular law along with its penalty—the law that made adultery a civil crime rather than just a religious sin. Remember that Korihor, as part of his religious philosophy, endorsed adultery. He thought that he should be free to commit adultery without penalty if his religious beliefs allowed it. Korihor, like so many other apostates throughout history, created a religion that would allow him to do *without* penalty that which God had forbidden as a choice *with* a penalty. "And thus he [Korihor] did preach unto them, . . . leading away many women, and also men, to commit whoredoms" (Alma 30:18).

Korihor's true motive for criticizing the Nephite government was that he did not want to be punished for committing adultery. Korihor probably would not have objected if the law forbade adultery, as long as it was not enforced with any penalty. Because there was a penalty attached to the law he wanted to break, he claimed that he and the people were in bondage. Hence, Korihor's definition of "free" was to have choice without penalty. Korihor used a philosophy similar to Satan's during the War in Heaven. Korihor, like Satan, tried to change the meaning of freedom, but Alma would not compromise. Alma knew that freedom must include laws with penalties, even for some so-called religious laws.

Alternative Definitions of Freedom

The word "free" can mean many things, but we are mainly concerned here with the kind of freedom to which the scriptures refer to—what we call "free agency." Though the scriptures give more than one meaning to the word "free," the type of freedom that directly impacts our agency is the freedom that comes because of the Atonement of Christ. It is this freedom that gives us the ability to make choices that affect our salvation. The scriptures give us two definitions: (1) choice without penalty, and (2) choice without compulsion.

Political Freedom: Choice Without Penalty

Making choices without penalty is the kind of freedom often spoken of in the Book of Mormon. Virtually every one of the twenty-seven instances of the word "freedom" in the Book of Mormon refer to the cause of freedom associated with the liberty the people enjoyed as a nation. It was this political freedom, freedom from oppression, that Korihor wanted to redefine.

In the United States, we enjoy basically the same kind of political freedom today. Freedom of speech is just one example of our political freedoms. Here people are free to speak out, even against the government. We can make the choice to speak against the government *without* fear of penalty. Without freedom of speech there would still be no limit to our ability to choose to speak against the government;

people can and do speak against their governments even in countries where it is forbidden. The problem is that it gets them into trouble—it is choice *with* a penalty attached. In America we can make the same choice *without* the threat of a penalty. This is what we call political freedom, but it is only one kind of freedom.

Political Freedom Contrasted with Spiritual Freedom

Because "freedom" is so often used in a political context, it is easy to wrongly apply the same meaning to the word in its gospel context. Political freedom is not the same kind of freedom that is part of "free agency." In fact, the "free" in free agency is nearly opposite in meaning to being "free" in a free country. Because freedom in a so-called "free country" is understood to mean having choice without penalty, many have supposed that this is what freedom means when we talk about free agency. This is a very big mistake. Herein is one of the problems with understanding both free agency and the War in Heaven: it is a misunderstanding of what kind of freedom we are talking about. Political freedom and spiritual freedom are two different things. Being "free to choose" in the gospel sense is absolutely *not* a freedom to choose without penalty.

"Ye are free to act for yourselves—to choose the way of everlasting death or the way of eternal life" (2 Nephi 10:23). The penalty of everlasting death is clearly the result of one of the choices mentioned. If being free to act includes the freedom to "choose the way of everlasting death," then freedom, in the gospel context, cannot mean choice without penalty. Being free here means choice without compulsion. This is so because we are not compelled to make our choices in life, but we are still accountable for the consequences of those choices. "And whosoever will not come the same is not compelled to come; but in the last day it shall be restored unto him according to his deeds" (Alma 42:27).

Remember in the object lesson when I held out two hands with a penny in each hand? We learned that true freedom is not possible unless the results of the choices are different. Since freedom only exists when the results of alternative choices are different, it stands to reason that one gains more freedom as the results between choices become more and more different. This being the case, we have the most freedom when the results of our choices are opposite. Thus we are not only free to choose between "the way of everlasting death" and "the way of eternal life," but without "the way of everlasting death" as an option, we would not really be free to choose at all.

This is a key concept that many of our youth do not understand. Some of them think that when their parents impose penalties for making bad choices, their free agency has been taken away. What is worse is that some parents believe this as well.

The belief that Satan's plan was to force us to be righteous feeds into this misunderstanding about freedom. Some wrongly suppose that agency is no more than the right to choose, and that this right is not only universal, but also without condition. They therefore conclude that agency must also be without penalty. From there, it is mistakenly assumed that anyone administering a penalty for a bad choice is violating someone's free agency. Many offenders believe that the mere threat of a penalty for a wrong choice means that they are being forced to make a "right" choice. This thinking is simply incorrect.

The philosophies of the world today fuel this falsehood by promoting the notion that freedom always means choice without penalty. Such false doctrine insists that no penalty should be administered for so-called wrong choices simply because people have the right to make choices. They believe that if anyone (including God) threatens to impose a penalty for their choices, their rights have been violated. The truth is that the "free" in "free agency" is not without penalty and never has been—but it *is* without compulsion.

Spiritual Freedom: Choice Without Compulsion

In most cases, political freedom is choice without penalty, whereas spiritual freedom is choice without compulsion. The following is an example of spiritual freedom. God told Adam that he was *free* to eat from any tree in the garden.

> I, the Lord God, commanded the man, saying: Of every tree of the garden thou mayest *freely* eat, But of the tree of knowledge of good and evil, thou shalt not eat of it, nevertheless, thou mayest choose for thyself, for it is given unto thee; but, remember that I forbid it, for in the day thou eatest thereof thou shalt surely die. [Moses 3:16–17; emphasis added]

What did the Lord mean by saying that Adam could "freely" eat of every tree in the garden? Being "free" to partake of "every tree" must have included the tree of knowledge of good and evil. There was a penalty attached to partaking of that tree, and Adam was soon informed of it. But since there was a penalty attached to one of Adam's choices, being free to choose from "every tree" did not mean he could make every choice without penalty. So although Adam was forbidden to partake of the tree of knowledge of good and evil, the Lord said to him, "thou mayest chose for thyself, for it (the choice) is given unto thee." Thus it was understood that he could make his choices without compulsion, but not without penalty.

His freedom to choose did not require that he be informed of the penalty, it only required multiple choices with different results. Until

Chapter 3   ∽   WHAT IS FREEDOM?

Adam was informed of the penalty, his situation was like the object lesson with a penny in one hand and nothing in the other. Even without knowing the results of the choices, the student is technically free to choose without compulsion. This is the kind of freedom Jacob spoke of: "Therefore, cheer up your hearts, and remember that ye are *free* to act for yourselves—to choose the way of everlasting death or the way of eternal life" (2 Nephi 10:23; emphasis added).

Again, we are "free to act," meaning free to choose without compulsion, but we are certainly not free to choose without penalty. We shall see that in fact it is the presence of *both reward and penalty* that makes us free. This is divine freedom or spiritual freedom as brought about by the Atonement of Christ.

Act for Yourselves

Spiritual freedom means to be able to act without compulsion, that is, without being compelled or coerced into making choices. Notice that the scripture above also says that "ye are free to act *for yourselves*," as opposed to acting for another.

Anciently, many people often acted *for another* because they were subject to a king, lord or master. When sent by a king to perform a certain task, a servant was acting *for the king* rather than for himself. When acting according to the king's commands, he was doing the king's business, and the king got the credit or the blame for the consequences of the task being performed. If a servant ever became free, he could then act *for himself*, but this also meant that he was responsible for the consequences his own decisions. He could no longer blame someone else if something went wrong. For a former servant, being free to act for himself did not mean that he could act without penalty, only that he could act without compulsion. Many penalties still applied if he acted wrongly. So it is when we act for ourselves today.

Three Elements of Spiritual Freedom

The freedom we are discussing now is spiritual freedom. There are three principles to observe about this kind of freedom: (1) it is available only because of the Atonement of Christ, (2) it is without compulsion, and (3) it includes the possibility of penalty.

Look carefully for all three of these elements of spiritual freedom in the following verses:

> And the Messiah cometh in the fulness of time, that he may redeem the children of men from the fall. And *because that they are redeemed* from the fall they have become *free* forever, knowing good from evil; to *act for themselves* and *not to be acted upon*, save it be by the *punishment* of the law at the great and last day, according to the commandments which God hath given.
>
> Wherefore, men are *free* according to the flesh; and all things are given them which are expedient unto man. And they are *free* to choose liberty and eternal life, *through the great Mediator* of all men, or to choose *captivity* and *death*, according to the captivity and power of the devil; for he seeketh that all men might be miserable like unto himself. [2 Nephi 2:26–27; emphasis added]
>
> And *under this head* ye are made *free*, and there is no other head whereby ye can be made *free*. There is no other name given whereby salvation cometh; therefore, I would that ye should take upon you the name of Christ. [Mosiah 5:8; emphasis added]

Principle 1—Freedom comes because of the Atonement of Christ. This is established by the following statements: "*Because that they are redeemed* from the fall they have become *free* forever," "they are *free* to choose liberty and eternal life, *through the great Mediator* of all men," and "*under this head* ye are made *free*."

Chapter 3   What Is Freedom?

Principle 2—Freedom is without compulsion. This is established by these statements: "To *act for themselves* and *not to be acted upon*," "men are *free* according to the flesh," and "they are *free* to choose."

Principle 3—Freedom includes the possibility of penalty. This is established thus: "To act for themselves and not to be acted upon, save it be by the *punishment* of the law and "they are *free* to choose . . . *captivity* and *death*."

Freedom Through the Atonement

How does the Atonement provide freedom? Wouldn't we still be free to choose even if there was no Atonement? The answer is no. We would still have choices without the Atonement, but not freedom. The reason why is because only through the Atonement do we have different results from our choices. This is explained by Jacob:

> Save it should be an infinite atonement this corruption could not put on incorruption. . . . And if so, this flesh must have laid down to rot and to crumble to its mother earth, to rise no more. . . . If the flesh should rise no more our spirits must become subject to that angel who fell. . . . And our spirits must have become like unto him, and we become devils, angels to a devil, to be shut out from the presence of our God, and to remain with the father of lies, in misery, like unto himself. [2 Nephi 9:7–9]

Without the Atonement we could still make whatever choices we wanted, good or bad, wicked or righteous, but it would all be for nothing. We could *be* good, but it wouldn't *do* any good. Regardless of all our best efforts to qualify for heaven, we would have all been doomed to hell, to spend eternity in misery with Satan. In other words, there would have been nothing but penalty regardless of our choices. Our *choices* would not have been limited without the Atonement, but the *results* of our choices would have. There is only one result for all of us without the Atonement: we all go to hell—we all suffer eternal death.

So the Atonement makes us free, *not* by increasing the number of choices, but by increasing the number of results. It is because of the Atonement that a different result from eternal death becomes possible: eternal life. Eternal life is only possible because of the Atonement, not because of *our* choices. This is why it is *by* grace and not *by* our works that we are saved. Our works are only important now that Christ has made an atonement, offering us different results for different choices. In other words, doing good now *does* some good, thanks to Him. He has done His part, and now it is up to us to do ours by choosing good rather than evil. Doing good can now result in eternal life because the Atonement has made eternal life a possibility.

Remember the part in the object lesson where each hand held a penny? The student was not really free to choose because the results of his choices were the same. In a condition without the Atonement, each penny represents hell. No matter which hand is chosen, hell is the result. When there was a penny in one hand and nothing in the other, the student became free because the results of his choices were different. Likewise, because the Atonement brings about the possibility of a reward, there is now "a law . . . upon which all blessings are predicated—and when we obtain any blessing from God, it is by obedience to that law upon which it is predicated" (D&C 130:20–21).

Free to Choose Means Free to Lose

The Atonement did not eliminate the possibility of penalty; it added the possibility of reward. Therefore, penalty still exists as a possible result even in the "merciful plan of the great creator." Just as darkness exists until light is introduced and cold exists unless heat is generated, a condition with penalty exists naturally, while a condition with reward must be provided. Alma's son Corianton sought for a condition *without* penalty. He had committed serious sexual transgressions and thought it was unjust for the sinner to suffer a penalty (Alma 42:1). In response, Alma taught him about the laws of justice and mercy and then asked this profound question: "How could there be a law save there was a punishment?" (Alma 42:17).

Since we cannot have law without penalty and it is laws that make us free, we cannot have freedom without the possibility of penalty. Therefore, as we learned in the object lesson with the pennies, to have freedom we must have different results from our choices, including penalties. Spiritual freedom then is created by having different results from our choices. Thus the principle of having "opposition in all things" (2 Nephi 2:11) applies not only to having opposite choices but to having opposite results as well.

The diabolical brilliance of Satan's plan can now become clear. If our freedom is destroyed by having a situation which brings only penalty and no reward, then the reverse situation must destroy freedom as well. *If we eliminate the option of penalty and thus have only rewards as the result of every choice, then different results would not exist and freedom would also be lost.* This is the key to Satan's plan. By this means comes the destruction of freedom, and therefore the destruction of the agency of man (Moses 4:3). *We must be free to lose or we cannot be free to choose.* It is a simple principle once understood, but it can be very hard to learn.

Chapter 4

What Is Agency?

The Importance of Understanding Agency

A misunderstanding of the meaning of agency has been the cause of a great deal of trouble within the families of the Latter-day Saints. It is fair for children to expect their parents to honor their agency. However, the belief of children (or parents) that agency is choice without penalty can be a formula for disaster. The contention over the meaning of agency did not start here. Twice the scriptures tell us that agency was the very principle over which the War in Heaven was fought (D&C 29:36; Moses 4:3). That war is not over, it has just changed battle grounds. Furthermore, agency is still the key issue, although Satan has done a masterful job of disguising it.

Many souls are still being lost. In the first round of this battle, the winners outnumbered the losers two to one (D&C 29:36; Revelation 12:4). Now the losers far outnumber the winners. Speaking of the proportion of winners to losers, Jesus said, "few there be that find it" (Matthew 7:14; D&C 132:22). Since all of this conflict and trouble is still about agency, understanding the true meaning of agency is essential if we are to know what we are fighting for, why some people are winning and why some people are losing this war.

As Latter-day Saints if we do not know the meaning of the cause we are fighting for, how valiant are we going to be as warriors? How likely is it that we will win a war if the very meaning of the cause is obscure? Finding the true meaning of agency is not an exercise in trivia, nor is it merely a matter of definition; it is fundamental to the entire cause for which we continue this war against the powers of darkness. Knowing the true meaning of agency will expose the efforts of Satan in ways never before known, but it is only the first step in winning the fight.

This is not to suggest that unless you can recite the formula of agency you will be going to hell. But the definition of agency does contain fundamental principles of the plan of salvation that must be understood before they can be properly applied. A thorough knowledge of the principles of agency will enable all of us to better understand the fall, the Atonement, and the entire plan of salvation. The principles of agency are those upon which the order of the priesthood is set and the reason the Church is organized as it is. Understanding agency teaches us to govern ourselves, our children and all those within our stewardships.

Since the message of this book depends upon establishing a better definition of the word "agency" than the one most people are familiar with, we will need to spend a little time on it. In anticipation of those who may not be willing to part with the old definition, there should be enough detail here to make it clear that agency is more than the right to choose.

Chapter 4 ~ WHAT IS AGENCY?

Agency = Stewardship

Ask Latter-day Saint teenagers what agency is and the answers will vary, but most will say something like "agency is the freedom to do whatever you want." The truth is we *can* do whatever we want, but that is *choice* or *freedom*, not agency. Agency includes three elements: choice, freedom, and sufficient knowledge to be accountable. Thus agency is responsibility, accountability and stewardship. This meaning can be established by a study of the dictionary definition of the word "agency," it's connection to the word "stewardship" and it's use in modern scripture.

The word "agency" is related to the word "agent." An agent is someone with responsibilities who represents someone else in the decisions he makes. For example, an employee is an agent. He represents his company, does the company's business, acts for and in behalf of the company and is accountable to that company for his acts. The word "agent" is found in modern scripture but not in the Bible. The Bible mentions people who act as agents, but the word used to identify them is "steward," so an agent and a steward are the same thing.

The business and responsibility of a steward is called his stewardship. *The business and responsibility of an agent is called his agency.* An agent is responsible and accountable for the choices he makes as an agent, just as a steward is responsible and accountable for the choices he makes as a steward.

Dictionary Definitions of Agency

If we are to figure out how Satan "sought to destroy the agency of man" (Moses 4:3), we need to know exactly what "agency" is. Since the definition we are seeking refers to the word as used in the Doctrine and Covenants and the Book of Moses in the 1830s, I chose to use Webster's 1828 dictionary. Like most words, both "agent" and "agency" have more than one definition. Though it cannot be denied that agency sometimes refers to the power to act or choose, the intent here is to show that in modern scripture it refers to stewardship and accountability.

The 1828 definition of the word "agent" is "a substitute, or deputy; one entrusted with the business of another." This refers to someone who is assigned to and responsible for certain duties. It appears that this is the definition of "agent" in the Doctrine and Covenants because all fifteen times it is used it refers to someone having some kind of responsibility. All but one refers to people who are accountable to other people. The one exception refers to our being accountable to God (D&C 29:35). In other words, an agent is a steward, someone who is accountable to someone else for the choices he makes.

It stands to reason that since the word "agent" refers to someone who is accountable, then its companion word "agency" must refer to their accountability. The 1828 dictionary confirms this. The definition for the word "agency" is "the office of an agent, business of an agent entrusted with the concerns of another." This definition describes the accountability and stewardship of an agent. In fact, in the 1828 Webster's Dictionary there is an old, unused synonym for stewardship: "agentship." The definition of "agentship" is identical to that of "agency." It is "the office of an agent." The dictionary then says, "[Not used.] We now use agency." Therefore "agency" is a shortened version of the word "agentship" and carries the same meaning. The evolution of the word appears to have gone from the word *stewardship*, to *agentship*, to *agency*. Agency then is much more than just being free to choose; *it is stewardship* and accountability. The question remaining is whether or not this is the definition the Lord intended in modern scripture? A review of a few scriptures will reveal that it is.

Stewards in Ancient Scripture

Ancient scriptures show the relationship between stewardship and accountability as well as modern scriptures do. In the New Testament several different Greek words are translated as either "steward" or "stewardship." Among the various meanings of these words in Strong's Greek Dictionary are, "to manage or a manager," "administration," "an overseer," or "a fiscal *agent*." The scriptures also make it clear that a steward is a person who is appointed to a certain measure of responsibility and accountability. "And the Lord said, Who then is that faithful and wise *steward*, whom his lord shall make ruler over his household, to give them their portion of meat in due season?" (Luke 12:42; emphasis added). And again: "There was a certain rich man, which had a *steward*. . . . And he called him, and said unto him, . . . give an *account* of thy *stewardship*; for thou mayest be no longer *steward*" (Luke 16:1–2; emphasis added). In 1 Corinthians 4:1–2 we find, "Let a man so *account* of us, as of the ministers of Christ, and *stewards* of the mysteries of God. Moreover it is *required* in *stewards*, that a man be found faithful" (emphasis added).

Stewards and Agents in Modern Scripture

The Doctrine and Covenants also shows the inseparable connection between stewardship and accountability. For instance, Doctrine and Covenant 42:32 says the following: "Every man shall be made *accountable* unto me, a *steward* over his own property" (emphasis added). Section 72 teaches us that the principle of accountability is an eternal one and applies even beyond our stewardships here on earth: "It is *required* of the Lord, at the hand of every *steward*, to render an *account* of his *stewardship*, both in time and in eternity" (v. 31; emphasis added).

The principle of accountability is applied to an agent in modern scripture the same as it was to a steward in ancient scripture. Notice also that since the bishop *is* the agent who keeps the storehouse and is the steward over temporal things, "agent" must be another word for "steward."

> I, the Lord, have *appointed* them, and ordained them to be *stewards* over the revelations; . . .
>
> And an *account* of this *stewardship* will I require of them in the day of judgement.
>
> Behold, this is what the Lord requires of every man in his *stewardship*, even as I, the Lord, have *appointed*. . . .
>
> And behold, none are exempt from this law who belong to the church. . . .
>
> Yea, neither the *bishop*, neither the *agent* who keepeth the Lord's storehouse, neither he who is *appointed* in a *stewardship* over temporal things. [D&C 70:3–4, 9–11; emphasis added]

Virtually every use of the word "agent" in the Doctrine and Covenants refers to someone who is appointed to a certain responsibility and is therefore accountable for his decisions therein. The following is another example: "He should also employ an *agent* to *take charge* and to do his secular *business* as he shall direct" (D&C 84:113; emphasis added). Just like a steward, an agent is appointed to a certain business for which he is responsible. In a spiritual sense, he is appointed to that business by the Lord to whom he is accountable. "Wherefore, as ye are *agents*, ye are on the Lord's *errand*; and whatsoever ye do according to the will of the Lord is the Lord's *business*" (D&C 64:29; emphasis added).

Chapter 4 ~ WHAT IS AGENCY?

The Lord's Definition of Agency

The scriptures we have read show that an agent and a steward are the same thing, so it stands to reason that "agency" and "stewardship" are also the same. But in the search to verify this, our objective should not be to attach *our own* definition to agency but to find out what *the Lord* meant when He used it.

The word "agency" is not used in the Bible and is used only six times in modern scripture. As it turns out, the occurrence least known is the one which makes the meaning most clear. In the other occurrences the meaning could be interpreted to be either definition we have offered, free choice *or* accountability. One scripture is an exception. In Doctrine and Covenants 57:6 Sidney Gilbert is appointed an agent in the land of Zion, specifically to "receive moneys . . . [and] to buy land." A few sections later the definition of agency is made clear: "It is expedient in me that my servant Sidney Gilbert, after a few weeks, shall return upon his *business*, and to his *agency* in the land of Zion" (D&C 64:18; emphasis added).

What was Sidney Gilbert being told to return to, his free choice or his stewardship? It makes no sense if agency refers to Sidney's free choice; to return to it, he would need to have left it somewhere. If a person cannot leave his free choice, he certainly cannot return to it. Therefore *agency* must refer to his *stewardship*, the business for which he was responsible and accountable. The next question is does this definition apply to the other scriptures that use the word "agency"?

Agency = Accountability

Other scriptures actually strengthen the case for this definition of agency. Notice the following connection between agents, accountability, and stewardship. "*Appoint* every man his *stewardship*; That every man may give an *account* unto me of the *stewardship* which is *appointed* unto him. For it is expedient that I, the Lord, should make every man *accountable*, as a *steward* over earthly blessings. . . . I . . . have given unto the children of men to be *agents* unto themselves" (D&C 104:11–13, 17; emphasis added).

The meaning of the expression "agents unto themselves" can be misleading. It does not mean that we are accountable *to* ourselves, but rather *for* ourselves. As an "agent *unto* the church," Sidney Gilbert acted *for* the Church and was accountable *to* the Church (D&C 57:6). The Church was also responsible for the consequences of Sidney's decisions. As agents *unto* ourselves we act *for* ourselves and are responsible for the consequences of our own decisions, thus expressing the old law of the harvest that "whatsoever a man soweth, that shall he also reap" (Galatians 6:7). The phrase "agents unto themselves," referring to the principle of personal accountability, was expressed in a similar way by Samuel the Lamanite: "Whosoever perisheth, perisheth *unto* himself; and whosoever doeth iniquity, doeth it *unto* himself; for behold, ye are free; ye are permitted to act *for* yourselves; for behold, God hath given unto you a knowledge and he hath made you free" (Helaman 14:30; emphasis added).

Being permitted to "act *for*" ourselves is the same as being "agents *unto*" ourselves. It is more than mere freedom. It includes accountability for the results of our choices so that "whosoever doeth iniquity, doeth it *unto* himself."

Freedom + Knowledge = Agency = Accountability

Notice in the verse just quoted that we are permitted to "act for" ourselves because of two stated conditions: God has given us knowledge and He has made us free. These conditions, however, are not always present at the same time. It is possible to be free to make choices and not have sufficient knowledge to be accountable for them. Thus it is possible to be free and still not have agency. When scriptures speak only of our freedom to choose they use words such as "free," "freedom," "choice," "choose," "decision," or "act." The word "agency" is more. It includes having sufficient knowledge to make us accountable. "That every man may *act* in doctrine and principle pertaining to futurity, according to the moral *agency* which I have given unto him, that every man may be *accountable* for his own sins in the day of judgement" (D&C 101:78; emphasis added).

Accountability comes not just because we can "act," but because we can act with sufficient knowledge of good and evil. Mentally handicapped people and little children can "act," but they have limited accountability because they lack sufficient knowledge of right and wrong (D&C 29:47–50). Since it is "moral agency" which makes every man "accountable for his own sins," moral agency must include having knowledge of good and evil. Therefore "moral agency" is more than moral freedom; it is moral accountability. This is why it is agency, not mere choice or freedom, that makes condemnation possible: "Behold, here is the *agency* of man, and here is the *condemnation* of man; because that which was from the beginning is plainly manifest unto them, and they receive not the light" (D&C 93:31; emphasis added). Here it is shown that both agency and condemnation exist when things are "plainly manifest" unto man.

Merely making choices, does not require that things be plainly manifest. People with mental limitations can make choices but are spared any condemnation because of the Atonement (Mosiah 3:11). It is when things are "plainly manifest" that people become accountable, so it is accountability, or in other words agency, that makes condemnation possible. Condemnation comes only when people act against their knowledge of good and evil. Agency then, must require a knowledge of good and evil in order to bring about condemnation. This being the case, agency is more than choice or freedom, neither of which requires a knowledge of good and evil. Agency is accountability that comes with knowledge. Agency, or accountability grows as knowledge of right and wrong increases. That is why the Lord explained, "I gave unto them their *knowledge*, in the day I created them; and in the Garden of Eden, gave I unto man his *agency*" (Moses 7:32; emphasis added).

God wanted Adam and Eve to have more than just the freedom to choose, He wanted them to be accountable for their choices. For this reason God gave them more than just choices. He gave them a knowledge of what was permitted, what was forbidden, and the different consequences of each choice (Moses 3:17). Having that knowledge, Adam and Eve had their stewardship, and they became accountable—they had agency.

Remember the part of the object lesson when I held out two hands, having a penny in one hand and nothing in the other? When the student did not know which hand held the penny, the choice was a matter of pure chance. If the only thing at stake is a penny, then it is no big deal. But if the penny represents heaven and having no penny represents hell, then making the right choice is a very big deal. Making a wrong choice by random chance and then being doomed to hell for it is no more fair than making the right choice by pure luck and being exalted to heaven.

The scriptural word for unfairness is "injustice." Since God is a just God, the notion that man would forever be held accountable for the choices he makes without a knowledge of the results of those choices is contrary to God's nature. God cannot and will not commit an injustice. If He did so, then God would cease to be God (Alma 42:13). Therefore, it is the eternal law of justice which demands that a basic knowledge of good and evil be given to all mankind so that we may all be held accountable according to the knowledge that we have. A basic knowledge of good and evil *is* given to all men. It is called the light of Christ (Moroni 7:16–18).

The Three Elements of Agency

A knowledge of good and evil is the third element of agency. The first is choice, which is obtained by having two or more options. The second is freedom, which is obtained by having different results from the options. Agency is having choice with freedom as is provided by different results, and then having a knowledge of those results.

Elder Bruce R. McConkie wrote that agency required three elements. Although he listed them in a different order and stated them a little differently, each can be compared to one of those in the formula given here. "All of the terms and conditions of the Lord's eternal plan operate because man has his agency, and none of it would have efficacy, virtue, or force if there were no agency. Agency requires opposites; agency demands freedom of choice; *agency decrees personal accountability for sin*" (Bruce R. McConkie, *A New Witness for the Articles of Faith* [1985], 89; emphasis added).

The first two elements discussed above—having two options with different results—are explained by Elder McConkie as having "freedom of choice" and requiring "opposites." These two principles of agency are more commonly known than the last one, that of "personal accountability," but there is no doubt that it must be present.

Elder Dennis B. Neuenschwander of the Quorum of the Seventy has also recognized that agency must have these same three elements. He stated, "What is the agency of man but the right to make choices within a framework of opposition and the assumption of responsibility for those choices?" (Dennis B. Neuenschwander, "The Path of Growth," *Ensign*, Dec.1999, 15).

Let us look carefully at his definition and compare it to our object lesson with the pennies. He first said that agency is the "right to make choices," which, as we know, requires two or more options. Next he said that these choices must be made "within a framework of opposition." In other words, the results of the choices must be different. If there is a penny in each hand, the results are the same and there is no real choice. Finally, Elder Neuenschwander said that there must be an "assumption of responsibility" for the choices. We become responsible for the consequences of our choices by having a sufficient knowledge of those consequences. Regardless of how it is stated, when agency is present, those three elements always exist to one degree or another.

Free Agency Isn't Free

When it becomes clear that accountability is an inseparable part of the definition of agency, then it can be seen that free agency is not as free as many think. If "being free" is understood to mean "choice without cost" or "choice without penalty," then there is really nothing free about it. Free agency is only free in the sense that choices are made without compulsion.

Although the term "free agency" is not a scriptural expression, there is nothing wrong with using it. It does, however, need to be understood correctly. The word "free" refers to our freedom to make different choices without compulsion, and the word "agency" refers to our eternal accountability for the differing results of those choices. Because this has not always been clearly understood, many of those who *do* understand have begun using alternative words like "agency" or "moral agency."

Chapter 4 ~ WHAT IS AGENCY?

The Damning Doctrine of Unaccountability

Regardless of the words being used, Church leaders have certainly put a greater emphasis on the principle of accountability in recent years. There is scarcely a talk given without mention of it. The brethren are well aware that some people are quick to demand their freedom and rights but slow to accept responsibility for their actions. The meaning of the word "freedom" has been so twisted that many believe it is their right to act without being accountable for their actions. Many foolish decisions are made without regard to the eternal and irrevocable consequences of those decisions. "They seek not the Lord to establish his righteousness, but every man walketh in *his own* way, and after the image of *his own* god" (D&C 1:16; emphasis added).

Many do as they please and then expect to have what they want, but since "wickedness never was happiness" (Alma 41:10), they will continue to fail. The doctrine of unaccountability is completely contrary to the nature and will of God and His plan for the happiness of man. The message of the scriptures is that man is responsible and accountable when making choices. "Who am I that made man, saith the Lord, that will hold him guiltless that obeys not my commandments? Who am I, saith the Lord, that have promised and have not fulfilled?" (D&C 58:30).

It is the nature of the natural man to believe or hope that he will be held guiltless regardless of what he does. The desire to avoid accountability is the root that feeds the lusts of mankind. Lusts drive the natural man to satisfy the "will of the flesh" (2 Nephi 2:29), which is why "they seek not the Lord to establish *his* righteousness," and why "every man walketh in *his own* way, and after the image of *his own* god" (D&C 1:16; emphasis added). Can you guess who might be the author of all this falsehood? If you thought of Satan, you were right. Obviously then the conflict didn't start here on earth. Elder Neuenschwander identified personal responsibility as the issue over which the War in Heaven was fought. "The battle over *responsibility* is a familiar one, and it reaches back far into the past even before our mortal existence. To Moses, the Lord revealed that Satan 'sought to destroy the *agency* of man,'" ("The Path of Growth," *Ensign,* Dec. 1999, 15; emphasis added).

Elder Neuenschwander said that the War in Heaven was a battle over *responsibility.* This is exactly what is meant when the scripture says that Satan "sought to destroy the agency of man" (Moses 4:3). *The question is how?* How could Satan's plan have destroyed our responsibility or stewardship? Forcing us to be righteous certainly would have destroyed our personal responsibility, but is that the only way to do it? Since there are at least three elements to agency, wouldn't the elimination of any one of the three elements effectively destroy it? The authors of the 1999 Old Testament Seminary Manual thought so. They not only acknowledged that the "force plan" is "only one possibility" for destroying agency, but they also conceded that eliminating any one of the conditions of agency would destroy it. They wrote: "Most people think that he [Satan] would have *forced* us to do right, but that is *only one possibility.* Certain conditions are necessary if we are to have agency. . . . Satan might have destroyed our agency by eliminating any one of those [conditions] and he is still trying to destroy our agency using the *same* techniques of deception and lies" (1999 CES Teacher Resource Manual, 27; emphasis added).

Seminary manuals, as official publications of the Church, are fairly well scrutinized before they are approved. This quote questions the old "force plan" and opens the door to exploring other options.

At this point it becomes clear that there is something about the

Chapter 4 ~ WHAT IS AGENCY?

War in Heaven which Satan does not want us to know. The one thing a deceiver cannot survive is exposure. Exposing Satan's plan is exactly what a correct understanding of agency will do. What is it that Satan doesn't want us to know about the War in Heaven?

Chapter 5

From Lucifer to Perdition

Lucifer the Morning Star

In order to expose Satan and his plan it is important to examine the causes of his fall—his motivation to develop an alternate plan and lead a futile rebellion against God.

Joseph Smith and Sidney Rigdon saw in vision the rebellion of Lucifer, his fall from grace and his banishment after the War in Heaven.

> And this we saw also, and bear record, that an angel of God who was in authority in the presence of God, who rebelled against the Only Begotten Son, . . . was thrust down from the presence of God and the Son, And was called Perdition, for the heavens wept over him—he was Lucifer, a son of the morning. [D&C 76:25–26]

The saddest part of Satan's fall is the fact that he was once "in authority in the presence of God." We do not know how long he enjoyed his status as a noble and great one, nor do we know what role he might have played on earth if he had continued faithfully. We get only a small sense of the tragedy when we read that "the heavens wept over him" (D&C 76:26).

In scripture it appears "Lucifer" was the name by which he was known before his fall, and that "Perdition" was one of the name-titles given to him afterwards (D&C 76:26). Perdition comes from a Greek word meaning "ruin, loss, destruction, waste" (*Strong's Exhaustive Concordance of the Bible*—Greek Dictionary [Kansas City, 1984], 15), all of which describe the Satan we are familiar with. But he wasn't always spoken of in such derogatory terms.

"Lucifer" was a noble and honorable name consistent with his previous position of authority in the presence of God. It is actually a word meaning "brightness, morning star," (*Strong's Exhaustive Concordance of the Bible*—Hebrew and Chaldee Dictionary, [1984], 32) a very complimentary description of a being with great "intelligence, or, in other words, light and truth" (D&C 93:36). Surely, in the presence of God, Lucifer enjoyed "the light of truth; which truth shineth" (D&C 88:6–7). "Stars," in scripture, often refer to sons of God, whether good or evil (Job 38:7; Revelation 12:4). Just as the morning is the beginning of the light of day, a "morning star" is a son of God who was "in the beginning with God," such as Christ (John 1:1–2), as well as others (Job 38:7). Lucifer was among them and in authority in the presence of God. He "is the same which was from the beginning" (Moses 4:1). He was Lucifer, a bright morning star.

It is interesting to note that Christ speaks of himself in these very same terms: "I Jesus . . . am . . . the bright and morning star" (Revelation 22:16). Lucifer, therefore, must have once possessed many of the divine attributes that Christ has. He must have been admired, respected, honored and loved. No wonder "the heavens wept over him" (D&C 76:26).

What could cause the fall of such a great and noble being? What could have influenced a once great and noble being to become so angry, hateful and willfully evil? His rebellion appears to have been sparked by the enticement of aspiration and then fueled by angry pride. Satan wanted a high position that he couldn't have and the glory and honor that came with it.

Lucifer Wanted to Be the Messiah

In the following scripture it is clear that Lucifer wanted to be the Messiah. Though he was certainly not able to accomplish the required suffering, he did want to be the one chosen to go to earth as the Only Begotten of the Father to make an atonement for all mankind. "Satan . . . came before me, saying— Behold, here am I, send me, I will *be thy son*, and I will *redeem* all mankind" (Moses 4:1; emphasis added).

Elder Bruce R. McConkie, in paraphrasing Satan's plan, indicated that he desired to be the Messiah. "That is: 'I reject thy plan. I am willing to be thy Son and atone for the sins of the world, but in return let me take thy throne'" (Bruce R. McConkie, *The Promised Messiah* [1978], 49–50).

This desire to be the Messiah was the beginning of the end for Lucifer. Father had chosen Jesus because He was the only one fully qualified (Revelation 5:3–5). Father's decision should have been accepted by Lucifer, but it was not.

When the Messiah Was Chosen

The Book of Revelation speaks of the time when the Messiah was chosen.

> And I saw in the right hand of him that sat on the throne a book written within and on the backside, sealed with seven seals.
>
> And I saw a strong angel proclaiming with a loud voice, Who is worthy to open the book, and to loose the seals thereof?
>
> And no man in heaven, nor in earth, neither under the earth, was able to open the book, neither to look thereon.
>
> And I wept much, because no man was found worthy to open and to read the book, neither to look thereon. [Revelation 5:1–4]

Explanations of the symbolism make these verses more clear. The Father is the one on the throne. The book in His right hand obviously represents something extremely important, so important that John wept because no one was worthy to open it or read it. The book, representing the mission of the Messiah, "contains the revealed will, mysteries, and the works of God; [and] the hidden things of his economy" (D&C 77:6), or in other words the plan of salvation. Just as the book could not be opened until someone worthy was found, the plan of salvation could not begin until someone was chosen to be the Messiah—someone who could and would fulfill the demands of the Atonement. The text continues to describe Christ as the only one worthy and chosen by the Father to accomplish the Atonement and complete the plan of salvation for all the human family.

> And one of the elders saith unto me, Weep not: behold, *the Lion of the tribe of Juda, the Root of David*, hath prevailed to open the book, and to loose the seven seals thereof.
>
> And I beheld, and, lo, in the midst of the throne . . . stood a *Lamb as it had been slain*. . . .
>
> And he came and took the book out of the right hand of him that sat upon the throne.

Chapter 6   From Lucifer to Perdition

> And when he had taken the book, the four beasts and four and twenty elders fell down before the Lamb. . . .
>
> And they sung a new song, saying, Thou art worthy to take the book, and to open the seals thereof: for *thou wast slain, and hast redeemed us to God by thy blood* out of every kindred, and tongue, and people, and nation. [Revelation 5:5–9; emphasis added]

It is not essential to discuss all of the symbolism seen above. The two most important things are that Jesus Christ is the "Lion of the tribe of Judah," and "the Root of David" who "prevailed to open the book" and that there are clear references to His Atonement in the phrases, "a Lamb as it had been slain" and "redeemed us to God by thy blood." The next important point is the rejoicing that John saw and heard from all of God's creations once the Messiah had been chosen.

> And I beheld, and I heard the voice of many angels round about the throne and the beasts and the elders: and the number of them was ten thousand times ten thousand, and thousands of thousands;
>
> Saying with a loud voice, *Worthy is the Lamb that was slain to receive power, and riches, and wisdom, and strength, and honour, and glory, and blessing.*
>
> And every creature which is in heaven, and on the earth, and under the earth, and such as are in the sea, and all that are in them, heard I saying, *Blessing, and honour, and glory, and power, be unto him that sitteth upon the throne, and unto the Lamb for ever and ever.* [Revelation 5:11–13; emphasis added]

The joy and rejoicing must have been tremendous. It was a celebration like no other. This is probably the event spoken of in Job "when the morning stars sang together, and all the sons of God shouted for joy" (Job 38:7). If "all the sons of God" were there, then

Lucifer was too. He surely witnessed all the rejoicing, the worship, and the honor given to the one chosen by Father to be the Savior.

Lucifer's Lust for Power

The seeds of envy were probably planted in Lucifer's heart shortly after the Messiah was chosen. Being in authority he was already the recipient of much honor and respect, but it was apparently not enough now that he saw the spotlight shining somewhere else. Nearly every account of the fall of Lucifer includes references to his desire for power.

> How art thou fallen from heaven, O Lucifer, son of the morning! . . .
>
> For thou hast said in thine heart, *I will ascend into heaven, I will exalt my throne above the stars of God:* . . .
>
> *I will ascend above the heights of the clouds; I will be like the most High.* [Isaiah 14:12–13; emphasis added]

> The devil . . . rebelled against me, saying, *Give me thine honor, which is my power.* [D&C 29:36; emphasis added]

> Satan, that old serpent, even the devil, who rebelled against God, and *sought to take the kingdom of our God and his Christ.* [D&C 76:28; emphasis added]

> Behold, *here am I, send me, I will be thy son,* and I will redeem all mankind, that one soul shall not be lost, and surely I will do it; wherefore *give me thine honor.* [Moses 4:1; emphasis added]

Often what motivates a person to aspire to high position is the honor and admiration that goes with it. Lucifer had witnessed the highest honor and praise ever given to any of the sons of God when Jesus was chosen to be the Messiah. He liked what he had seen and wanted it for himself. No doubt he first developed a plan before he made his move, saying, "Behold, here am I, send me, I will be thy son" (Moses 4:1).

Lucifer's Campaign Begins

Wanting to be "thy son" meant wanting to be the Messiah. The problem for Lucifer was that Jesus had been chosen because He was the only one qualified to enact the principles and laws of the Atonement and the plan of salvation as Father had outlined it. Therefore Lucifer could hardly offer himself as an alternative Messiah under the existing conditions. Like most political challengers, Lucifer knew that people would see no need for a new leader unless they were convinced of a need for new rules.

For scriptural examples of this, consider the case of Jeroboam, who took ten tribes away from Reoboam over taxation issues (1 Kings 12:1–19). The same applied when the children of Israel rebelled saying, "Let us make a captain, and let us return into Egypt" (Numbers 14:4). Their plan was to abandon Moses and get a new leader who would give them what they wanted. Lucifer, therefore, understanding the natural man, knew he had to offer an alternative plan of salvation in order to offer himself as an alternative Messiah.

We certainly do not know all the details of Lucifer's arguments in the pre-earth life. But since the "natural man is an enemy to God" (Mosiah 3:19) and Satan is God's greatest enemy, a study of today's power-hungry liars is probably a good indicator of Satan's methods. Since the greatest tyrants of history have been taught by "that same being who did plot with Cain" (Helaman 6:27), we can learn much about the teacher simply by observing his most talented students.

The word "devil" actually means "slanderer," thus John calls him "the accuser of our brethren" (Revelation 12:10). From this description it is certain that slanderous accusations were a part of Lucifer's attack.

But Father is a perfect being, so what could Satan have possibly accused Father of? We do not have to guess. We already know the war was about agency (D&C 29:36; Moses 4:3). Since we have seen that agency is stewardship and accountability, it is probable that the accusations had something to do with the degree to which Father holds people accountable. Anyone who says that they "cannot look upon sin with the least degree of allowance" (D&C 1:31) is an easy target for someone wanting to excuse people from responsibility for their actions. Offering to redeem all mankind is a clear attack on accountability, whatever the details may have been.

Chapter 6

The Appeal of Satan's Plan

An Error Corrected

We often make assumptions in the search for truth, but assumptions can also lead us to error. One relevant example should illustrate this point.

Since 1830 the Church has known that Satan offered a different plan to redeem all mankind (Moses 4:1). At some point an assumption was made that Jesus offered a better plan and that Father chose it, making Satan angry enough to rebel and cause the War in Heaven. The error in this account is in believing that *both* Jesus and Satan offered plans when in fact only Satan offered an alternative to Father's plan. The idea of two plans being presented may have come from a scripture which *does* show two opposing viewpoints: "Satan . . . came before me, saying—Behold, here am I, send me, I will be thy son, and I will redeem all mankind, that one soul shall not be lost. . . . But, behold my Beloved Son . . . said unto me—Father, thy will be done, and the glory be thine forever" (Moses 4:1–2). The assumption has been made that the two opposing viewpoints meant that there were two proposed plans, but the scriptures never state that Jesus offered a plan. Rather, they affirm that Jesus humbly accepted Father's plan.

Some very clear thinking and a closer look at the scriptures corrected this tradition. No one could stamp out a false tradition quite like Elder Bruce R. McConkie: "One of the saddest examples of a misconceived and twisted knowledge of an otherwise glorious concept is the all-too-common heresy that there were two plans of salvation; that the Father (presumptively at a loss to know what to do) asked others for proposals" (Bruce R. McConkie, *The Mortal Messiah*, 4 vols. [1979], 1:48 note 3).

Jesus did not propose anything new. He simply supported the plan that Father had already presented when he said, "Father, thy will be done, and the glory be thine forever" (Moses 4:2).

How Did We Get the "Force" Idea?

Most Latter-day Saints have also assumed for many years that Satan's plan was to force everyone to be righteous so that we could all be saved, an idea probably based on the account of the War in Heaven in Moses 4. But a careful reading of the account establishes no mention of anyone being forced. "Satan . . . came before me saying—Behold, here am I, send me, I will be thy son, and I will redeem all mankind, that one soul shall not be lost, and surely I will do it; wherefore give me thine honor. . . . Wherefore, because that Satan rebelled against me, and sought to destroy the *agency* of man, which I, the Lord God, had given him, . . . I caused that he should be cast down" (Moses 4:1, 3; emphasis added).

Since no scripture actually states that Satan intended to force us to do anything, there must have been some unwarranted assumptions to arrive at that conclusion. The logic probably went something like this: Since no unclean thing can enter into the kingdom of heaven mankind can only be saved if they are righteous (1 Nephi 15:34). Therefore since agency is the freedom to choose, and Satan promised to save all mankind by destroying this freedom, then his plan must have been to force us to be righteous.

The logic seemed to fit, so the assumption became tradition, and generations passed it on without question. The problem is that we had to fill in some doctrinal blanks to get there. If this tradition can be examined carefully and with an open mind, a much more subtle and deceptive plan will emerge.

A Rebellion of Compulsion or Persuasion?

It would make little sense to challenge an all-powerful being. All of God's children combined could never compel God to do something against His will. Otherwise He would not be all-powerful, as the scriptures state He is (Isaiah 10:15; 1 Nephi 4:1; Mosiah 4:9). If Satan or his followers *could* have taken Father's power, there is no doubt they *would* have, so obviously it was not possible, and they knew it. The War in Heaven was not an attempt to *compel* God to do anything. It was an attempt to *persuade* Him to do something. Scriptures indicate that Father was asked to *give* His honor and power to Satan. The scriptures state that Satan "rebelled against me, saying, *Give* me thine honor, which is my power" (D&C 29:36). And again, "Satan rebelled against me, and sought . . . that I should *give* unto him mine own power" (Moses 4:3). Since the scriptures state that Satan wanted God to *give* him His power, it seems clear that Satan knew he could not take it by force. Therefore, the rebellion against God was an attempt to persuade God to forfeit His power.

The power of God, which Satan wanted, is His stewardship as the supreme judge of mankind. We know this because Christ is subject to the Father and by virtue of His Atonement intercedes in our behalf, pleading to the Father to grant us salvation. "Listen to him who is the advocate with the Father, who is pleading your cause before him— Saying: Father. . . . spare these my brethren that believe on my name, that they may come unto me and have everlasting life" (D&C 45:3–5).

Who returns to His presence and who does not, is ultimately up to the Father. This is God's power and His honor. Therefore, Satan actually rebelled against *both* the Father and the Son (D&C 76:25; Moses 4:3) when he offered to be the Messiah and sought the power of God in redeeming "all mankind, that one soul shall not be lost" (Moses 4:1). So when Satan said: "give me thine honor" (v.1), it was an attempt to persuade God to forfeit His stewardship as the supreme judge over mankind.

What Motivated the Rebellion?

To attempt to persuade God to change His plan is to assume there *is* a flaw in the plan. Having a flaw in God's plan would require *imperfect* thinking from a *perfect* being. Such an arrogant suggestion could only come from someone hoping to outsmart God. But an attempt to outsmart an omniscient God doesn't seem any more logical than an attempt to overpower an omnipotent one. So no matter what Satan's thinking was, it wasn't very good thinking. Maybe that's why the scripture says that "he knew not the mind of God, wherefore he sought to destroy the world" (Moses 4:6). But now something else doesn't make sense.

If the rebellion against God demonstrated such poor judgement on Satan's part, how do we explain the fact that he was once "in authority in the presence of God" (D&C 76:25)? Lucifer was not stupid, yet he was certainly not smart to rebel against God. How can this apparent contradiction be explained? The answer comes in understanding the power of negative emotions. Typically, the more people allow negative emotions to control them, the more they lose their ability to control themselves through logical reasoning. We know that negative emotions motivated Lucifer's rebellion, because scripture states that he "was *angry*, and kept not his first estate" (Abraham 3:28; emphasis added). Anger is one of the strongest negative emotions, one that can easily blind the rational mind. Those who rebelled had to be far more emotional than rational because an attempt to either outsmart or overpower a perfect being is not logical. So in searching for the motivation behind Satan's plan, we must search for a proposal that has a lot of emotional appeal.

It is clear that Satan wanted power, but what motivated his followers? Scripture reveals that part of what motivated them was Lucifer's promise of guaranteed salvation, when he said, "I will redeem all mankind, that one soul shall not be lost" (Moses 4:1). That was the promised end, but what were the means needed in order to achieve it? The enticement of the promise of guaranteed salvation is obvious, but this is not the part of Satan's plan that is in question. *How* he proposed to bring about universal salvation is the question we are considering. Tradition has it that he proposed to force us to be righteous in order to provide universal salvation. But does that proposal stir up enough emotions to motivate billions to rebel against God? Whatever the proposal was, it had to be something that stirred their emotions sufficiently to motivate them to rebel against an omniscient and omnipotent God.

To a master deceiver, it is fairly easy to win a crowd. All you have to do is tell them what they want to hear. Samuel the Lamanite pointed out that the Gadiantons used this method with the Nephites: "If a man shall come among you and shall say . . . do whatsoever your heart desireth . . . ye will receive him, and say that he is a prophet"

(Helaman 13:27). Likewise, Satan's promise of guaranteed salvation would have gotten a lot of attention. But the natural questions on everyone's mind would have been: "What is the catch and what is it going to cost me?" There will be no sale if the price is too high. The force plan said the price of salvation was to agree to be forced into obedience. But what if the price of guaranteed salvation cost nothing at all? What could stir up a crowd more than to promise them exactly what they wanted, *and* at no charge? What could be more appealing than a city which offers new residents a dream house and a dream car for free? Now imagine your disappointment and anger when the national government says that such an offer is illegal. The people wanting to move to that city would be upset indeed.

The Story of the Three Universities

Consider the following hypothetical situation which creates insightful classroom discussion. Suppose that a group of high school seniors are preparing to go to college and representatives of three different schools are trying to recruit them. Afterwards each student must make a decision and vote on which of the three universities to attend.

Force College—The college representative explains that at Force College no one ever has, or ever will get into trouble on campus. No one ever breaks any rules. No one needs to worry about their safety or well being. There are security guards everywhere who do not allow anyone to break any rules or harm anyone else in any way. All students are forced to live the school's standards. Personal tutors force students to study and learn. As a result, everyone gets straight A's. Graduation and straight A's are absolutely guaranteed to every single person enrolled in Force College.

University of Freedom—The second recruiter explains that at the University of Freedom, "Do As You Please" is the school motto. The

Chapter 6 ~ THE APPEAL OF SATAN'S PLAN

only requirement is attendance on campus, though not necessarily in class. You may read, study, sleep, play, dance, talk, wander around, or just sit and listen to your music. There are absolutely no rules or restrictions. There are no standards of dress or conduct. You may wear what you please and do what you please whenever you please. If you wish to educate yourself, you are free to do so. Teachers are available if and when you need them. Books are also available in the library should you want to study. The campus entertainment center is always open, complete with everything you can imagine. The cafeteria is always open and the food is free. You may eat what, when, and as much as you wish. You are totally free to do as you please. They also guarantee you will receive straight A's, and every single student will graduate regardless of what you have or have not done.

Law School—The third recruiter describes Law School as a place where facilities and teachers are available only at certain times, and a strict schedule of classes is maintained. There are many rules of conduct which provide a safe and orderly environment to protect the rights of everyone. Obedience to the standards is expected and disobedience is punished. Learning is the purpose of this school and efforts toward learning are expected of all. No one will be compelled in any way either to study or to attend classes, but hard work and dependability will be rewarded while laziness will not. Generally, only a few excel, though all are free to do so. You are graded against certain standards and criteria but not against other students. You are free to succeed, fail, and be average. While straight A's and graduation are *possible* for every student, they are only given to those who meet the requirements.

Which School Represents Which Plan?

The younger the group to whom these choices are presented to, the greater percentage of them want to go to the University of

Freedom. The more immature the group, the more irresponsibly they vote. After the students vote, it is enlightening to let them debate the advantages of their choices with the objective of recruiting others to their school.

The University of Freedom group is usually hilarious. Listening to them attempt to explain how they are going to get as good an education at the University of Freedom as anywhere else must be heard to be believed. Although their arguments are not very rational, the appeal of the University of Freedom is intoxicating. What could be more enticing than an unconditional, no-risk guarantee? They get the same grade and diploma as the Force College students, but nothing is required of them to achieve it.

After they have debated the pros and cons of the different schools, it is time to ask some very important questions. First, which of the three schools best represents Father's plan for the salvation of mankind? Most recognize Law School as Father's plan because it preserves both choice and accountability.

The next question reveals the purpose of the story. Which of the two remaining schools, Force College or the University of Freedom, best represents Satan's plan? The immediate response is generally that Force College is the one, but after thinking about it, that answer loses its appeal. What Satan offers is usually very enticing. Force College is *not* very appealing, and the University of Freedom *is*, but the latter does not describe what we have heard about Satan's plan. To reconcile this, some suggest that Force College may represent Satan's plan in the pre-earth life, while the University of Freedom represents his plan here on earth. In other words, they were thinking that perhaps he changed plans.

Why would Satan have used a less enticing plan in the pre-earth life than what he uses on earth? People had more knowledge in the

Chapter 6 ~ THE APPEAL OF SATAN'S PLAN

pre-earth life than they do here on earth and would have been much more difficult to deceive. His proposal in the pre-earth life would have required an even more clever and subtle plan than what he uses here on earth. Force College is simply not enticing enough when compared to the University of Freedom.

The promise of reward with nothing required attracts the most irresponsible people. So it was in the War in Heaven. The more lazy, selfish, and prideful among us were surely the most easily persuaded. Then when Father denied their desire, their stubbornness grew into anger, even rage. Such powerful negative emotions were the fertile soil necessary to motivate people to rise up in rebellion against, and in defiance of an omniscient and omnipotent God.

What do the Scriptures Say?

Scriptures are so full of examples showing that Law School is like Father's plan, that quoting them is unnecessary. Father sets the standards by giving us commandments. He provides us choices by giving us the ability to act. He informs us of the consequences by making promises, and He holds us accountable by bringing us to judgement.

Scriptural parallels to Force College are difficult to find. The only time anyone was really forced to do anything was when they became possessed by evil spirits (Matthew 8:28–29; Mark 1:23–26; 5:1–5; 9:17–22). Only when possessed did people completely lose their ability to make their own choices. But even these instances are unlike Satan's plan because those who were possessed were being forced to do evil rather than good. There are examples of corrupt rulers in scripture, both civil and religious, but they never forced anyone, they compelled them. Even the few places where the word "force" is used in scripture do not refer to the kind of force that Satan's plan was going to impose. Compulsion is what is meant. To compel someone is to *pressure* them to make a choice. When forcing someone you *cause* them to make a choice. When forced to do something there is no other choice. So Satan's force plan is not really represented in the scriptures.

On the other hand, the University of Freedom is represented everywhere in scripture. From the Garden of Eden to the present, man has attempted to avoid accountability for his sins. It started with Adam and Eve's rather humorous attempt to hide from God among the trees in the Garden and cover their shame with fig leaves (Genesis 3:7–8). The rest of us down through history have done no better. To one degree or another, we all wear our own kind of fig leaves to cover our shame or try to find our own kind of trees in which to hide our guilt from God. It is all a vain attempt to avoid accountability. This human habit is nearly as common as sin itself.

Nephi understood that the natural man constantly tries to avoid accountability. In 2 Nephi 28 he gave a classic discourse on the wide variety of methods people use to avoid the consequences of sin. He said that many would "buil[d] up churches, and *not unto the Lord . . . and their priests . . . shall teach with their* learning" (2 Nephi 28:3–4; emphasis added). Why would anyone prefer *their own* learning over learning the truth about God? It is because God "cannot look upon sin with the least degree of allowance" (D&C 1:31). The natural man seeks to *allow* himself whatever degree of sin he is comfortable with. The problem with this is that true doctrine is inseparably connected with true commandments. So to reconcile the conflict between what God wants and what the natural man wants, either the natural man has to repent or the doctrines of God have to change.

The pure in heart are those whose beliefs are a higher priority than their behavior. They continually seek to modify their behavior, conforming it their beliefs. Contrast this to the natural man whose

Chapter 6 ~ THE APPEAL OF SATAN'S PLAN

first priority is his behavior. He will modify his beliefs to justify his behavior.

This explains the motive behind all apostasy from the true plan of salvation ever since the time of Adam. It is not really the doctrines that people don't like, it is the commandments connected to them. Jesus explained why it is that "men loved darkness rather than light." He said it was "because their deeds were evil" (John 3:19). He then continued, "For every one that doeth evil hateth the light, neither cometh to the light, *lest his deeds should be reproved*" (John 3:20; emphasis added).

Nephi has more examples of this key truth. Referring to false teachers, he writes: "they say unto the people: Hearken unto *us*, and hear ye *our* precept; for behold there is no God *today*, for the Lord . . . hath *done* his work, and he hath given his power unto men" (2 Nephi 28:5; emphasis added). Again, consider the motive behind a person who would create such false doctrine. It is to try to avoid accountability. Why "Hearken unto *us*, and hear ye *our* precept"? It is because then *we* get to make new rules, often by twisting the interpretation of the old ones. How can we justify this? Because if "there is no God *today*, for the Lord . . . hath *done* his work," you need *us* to tell you what to do. And we have the authority to do so because "he hath given his power unto men." This means that not only can we make rules we are comfortable with, but we also get to maintain power over people who look to us for instruction. You see, people create false religion first to justify their behavior, and secondly to satisfy their beliefs. They adopt false beliefs to justify wrong behavior and thus avoid accountability for it.

Nephi added that there are "many which shall say: Eat, drink, and be merry, for tomorrow we die; and it shall be well with us" (2 Nephi 28:7). What do they mean that it will be well with them, even after a lifetime of revelry? They mean that they believe God "will justify in committing a little sin" (v. 8). And why would God do that? Because, they say, "there is no harm in this" (v. 8). And just in case there is harm in this, they claim that "if it so be that we are guilty, God will beat us with a few stripes, and at last we shall be saved in the kingdom of God" (v. 8). This is a nicely packaged set of false beliefs, probably based upon some true aspect of God's nature such as His loving kindness and mercy. But this false doctrine ignores other aspects of God's character—that He is also a God of judgment and justice. The unrighteous reject the plain and precious doctrines that hold men accountable, such as:

> For behold, justice exerciseth all his demands, and also mercy claimeth all which is her own; and thus, none but the truly penitent are saved. What, do ye suppose that mercy can rob justice? I say unto you, Nay; not one whit. If so, God would cease to be God. [Alma 42:24–25]

Nephi continued, promising that "there shall be many which shall teach after this manner, false and vain and foolish doctrines" (2 Nephi 28:9). And what did Nephi say their motive is? It is to "seek deep to hide their counsels from the Lord" (v. 9). Why would anyone do this? Because "their works shall be in the dark" (v. 9). The Apostle Paul made the same observation about the relationship between beliefs and behavior, saying, "That they all might be damned who believed not the truth, but had pleasure in unrighteousness" (2 Thessalonians 2:12).

Nephi warned us: "Others he [Satan] flattereth away, and telleth them there is no hell; and he saith unto them: I am no devil, for there is none" (2 Nephi 28:22). It is obvious why this doctrine would be popular. If there is no devil and no hell, then there is no need to worry about the consequences of sin. But messengers of God have always taught the opposite, saying "nothing but repentance unto this

Chapter 6 ~ THE APPEAL OF SATAN'S PLAN

generation" (D&C 6:9). Jacob told his people that because "ye look upon me as a teacher, it must needs be expedient that I teach you the consequences of sin" (2 Nephi 9:48). Since nobody likes to be told the consequences of the sins they are committing, they often reject the message of repentance and create their own message, their own doctrines, their own religion.

Satan is obviously behind all this. Nephi also warned us that Satan shall "rage in the hearts of the children of men, and stir them up to anger against that which is good" (2 Nephi 28:20). Why would anyone be angry against that which is good? Jesus gave the answer, as he explained, "The world cannot hate you; but me it hateth, because I testify of it, that the works thereof are evil" (John 7:7). It is only the humble and penitent who do not mind being told they are wrong.

Nephi concedes that not everyone can be drawn into hatred. Satan has other techniques, but they are still based upon a desire to escape accountability. "And others will he pacify, and lull them away into carnal security, that they will say: All is well in Zion . . . and thus the devil cheateth their souls, and leadeth them away carefully down to hell" (2 Nephi 28:21). These people aren't hurting anybody are they? They are good people, so why should they be going to hell? It is because they believe that their goodness is good enough. This is false doctrine, which again is based upon *their own* comfort level of "righteous living."

If Jesus was serious when he said "be ye therefore perfect" (Matthew 5:48), then at what point in life can we sit back and say that we are good enough? King Benjamin taught that "if ye should serve him with all your whole souls yet ye would be unprofitable servants" (Mosiah 2:21). Remember that "it is by grace that we are saved *after all we can do*" (2 Nephi 25:23; emphasis added). Moroni said: "come unto Christ . . . and deny yourselves of all ungodliness ... *then* is his grace sufficient for you, that by his grace ye may be perfect in Christ" (Moroni 10:32; emphasis added). Only under the true doctrine of Christ do we find full and appropriate accountability. Any variation from the pure doctrine of Christ will introduce impurity and corruption.

The University of Freedom Is Satan's Plan

The loss of freedom is obvious at Force College. There is no deception about it, and *that* is the problem with it. The University of Freedom, on the other hand, does not limit choices at all. It does, however, limit the results of choices by eliminating the possibility of failure. Just like the part of the object lesson with a coin in each hand, the University of Freedom offers people choice, but no real freedom, and therefore no agency. The irony is that the students at the University of Freedom *think* they have more freedom than anyone else, but in reality they have none at all.

Remember that *if we are not free to lose, we are not really free to choose*. The deception at the University of Freedom is that people *think* they are free because they have so many choices. However, University of Freedom students don't seem to notice, or at least they don't care, that they have actually lost their freedom, since they get to do as they please and all their choices result in something desirable. They are not free to receive a different result, but they don't mind because the result being offered is something they want. Which plan do you think a master deceiver would use?

Chapter 7

Satan's Force Plan

As the story of the three universities illustrated, there are two major possibilities for Satan's plan. Force College represented a force plan, while the University of Freedom represented a freedom plan. To decide which one is more likely to have been Satan's plan, we need to take a closer look at both of them.

In the force plan Satan would have proposed to force us to be righteous. Under the force plan we could not choose evil since we would be forced to choose good. Since having a choice requires two or more options, the force plan destroys choice by eliminating all but one option. Destroying choice also destroys freedom as well as agency.

The Force Plan Is Not Scriptural

The first problem with the force plan is that the scriptures do not identify it as what was proposed. In fact, a careful look at the scriptures will give us a good reason to begin questioning it. In Moses 4:1, Lucifer is quoted as saying: "*I will be thy son, and I will redeem all mankind*, that one soul shall not be lost" (emphasis added).

If Lucifer was going to force us to never commit sin then why did he propose to redeem us? The very fact that he offered to redeem us casts some doubt on the force plan, because part of the reason we need a Messiah is to redeem us from sin. Under the force plan we would be sinless and thus qualified for heaven. The fact that Lucifer offered to redeem us shows that his plan probably included our freedom to sin.

The Force Plan Is Not Logical

Just how Lucifer would have forced us to be righteous is anybody's guess. It does not seem possible, but let us assume that somehow it is. Some have suggested that Lucifer, and presumably his followers, would have been able to force us by actually possessing our bodies. This makes little sense for at least three reasons.

First, Satan and his followers were more wicked than the rest of us who kept our first estate. This being the case, the force plan would require those who were most wicked among us, to force those who were more righteous to be even *more* righteous. Could or would wicked spirits force those who were more righteous than them to be perfectly righteous? Not likely, considering that Jesus said a corrupt tree cannot bring forth good fruit (Matthew 7:18).

Second, if Satan could force our bodies, our minds, our spirit and our very will to be righteous, then it would not be *us* being righteous at all, it would be *him*. How could this translate into our being righteous enough to qualify for heaven? The whole idea of forcing us to be righteous was to qualify *us* for salvation, but if our spirit or intelligence loses its individual will in the process of being forced, then our very consciousness is in question during the whole ordeal. This being the case, *we* would not have been righteous at all, for righteousness requires consciousness, "otherwise there is no existence" (D&C 93:30). This may be why President J. Reuben Clark questioned the possibility of a force plan. Speaking of Satan's plan he said: "I question whether the intelligence of man can be compelled" (J. Reuben Clark, Jr., in Conference Report, Oct. 1949, 193). If forcing us was not possible, would it have even been proposed?

Third, even if the evil spirits of Satan could somehow force us to be righteous, they could probably only force our bodies, rather than our minds or our hearts. Evidence for this is found in the New Testament account of a man possessed with many devils (Mark 5:1–15). Under their influence the man was living in tombs, cutting himself, and breaking chains with which he was bound. The devils had complete control of his body, *against his will*. After they were cast out, the man was said to be "in his right mind" (v. 15), suggesting that his mind had not been controlled, but only his body.

So Satan forcing us to be righteous would mean that we were being forced only into the actions of righteousness, performing the deeds of the law. The problem is that ritual righteousness is not enough for salvation, because yielding the mind and the heart (in other words the will of the individual spirit) is a large part of what righteousness is. "Behold, the Lord requireth the *heart* and a *willing mind*; and the willing *and* obedient shall eat the good of the land" (D&C 64:34; emphasis added).

The reason for this is given by Moroni:

> For behold, God hath said a man being evil cannot do that which is good; for if he offereth a gift, or prayeth unto God, except he shall do it with real intent it profiteth him nothing.
>
> For behold, *it is not counted unto him for righteousness.*
>
> For behold, if a man being evil giveth a gift, he doeth it grudgingly; wherefore it is counted unto him the same as if he had retained the gift; wherefore *he is counted evil before God.*

> And likewise also is it counted evil unto a man, if he shall pray and not with real intent of heart; yea, and *it profiteth him nothing*, for God receiveth none such.
>
> Wherefore, a man being evil *cannot do that which is good*; neither will he give a good gift. [Moroni 7:6–10; emphasis added]

If resentful righteousness is not counted as righteousness at all, then how much less would forced righteousness qualify? For instance, you could compel a boy scout to help old ladies cross the street, but he still might hate old ladies. Hating old ladies is not righteous, but you cannot force a boy scout to like them. Helping them cross the street is better than not helping them, but until the boy scout learns to have compassion for old ladies, helping thousands of them is not doing *him* much good. The Savior's Sermon on the Mount is all about going beyond ritual righteousness. There He taught us to become pure in heart and mind, not just in the actions of the body (Matthew 5–7).

So even if the force plan could have gotten us all back to heaven it could not have guaranteed that people would remain righteous or that they actually were righteous in their hearts at all. Learning to be righteous is not like learning a trade at Force College. Righteousness is not something you simply understand *how* to do, it is something you willingly *do*, and even more than that, it is something you *become*. It is much more than merely going through the prescribed motions. It is *voluntarily* doing good, not only in action, but in heart and in mind.

The Force Plan Is Not Appealing

The major flaw in the force plan is *not* that it is unworkable. Both force and freedom plans are unworkable. The biggest problem with the force plan is that its flaws are too obvious. If a proposed change in Father's plan of salvation is to have wide acceptance, the flaws in

Chapter 7 ~ SATAN'S FORCE PLAN

the plan must be very well hidden. The flaws in the force plan are too obvious for it to be deceptive enough to have gained wide acceptance.

Statements from our first parents, Adam and Eve, expose another flaw in the force plan. "Because of my transgression my eyes are opened. . . . Were it not for our transgression we . . . never should have known good and evil, and the joy of our redemption" (Moses 5:10–11).

The value of our experience in this world of transgression is that we can understand good and evil and have our eyes opened. In our "first estate," we were desirous of being "added upon," or making progress (Abraham 3:26). Forcing us to be righteous would have prevented all of us from committing sin and thus deprived us of having our eyes opened, from knowing the consequences of good and evil. We would not have known evil because we would never have seen or been exposed to sin. Jesus said "it must needs be that offences come" (Matthew 18:7). As the Lord explained to Joseph Smith, "All these things shall give thee experience, and shall be for thy good" (D&C 122:7).

We all knew from the beginning that we needed a redeemer, and we rejoiced when one was chosen (Revelation 5:1–14). We knew this was the only way for us to receive "the joy of our redemption" (Moses 5:11). Lucifer offered himself as a substitute redeemer because he understood that we needed redemption from sin. Therefore a plan that would have prevented us from sinning would have deprived us of the learning necessary for us to have "the joy of our redemption" (v. 11). This is another obvious flaw in the force plan, making it less likely that Lucifer would have made such a blunder.

The only potentially appealing part of the force plan was the end result, but now, we can see that even the end result has become unappealing because it deprives us of having our eyes opened and becoming as gods, "knowing good and evil" (Genesis 3:22; Moses 4:11). With the enticement of the force plan all but vanished, it becomes evident that it is not a likely scenario for Satan's plan. It is not clever or enticing. It breeds no rebellion. It is not worth a war.

A Brilliant Masterpiece of Deception

Having been "in authority in the presence of God" (D&C 76:25), Lucifer must have understood Father's plan of salvation. Possessing such a great intellect and knowledge of human nature, he surely would have conceived a plan which was as brilliant as he was. Such a plan would have to have met certain criteria. It would have to have been a masterpiece of deception, so brilliant that most people would see only its advantages, not the well-hidden flaws. It would have to have been so enticing as to stir up a rebellion against an all-powerful God. It would have to have been a plan that would destroy agency just as thoroughly as the force plan, but far less noticeably. There actually is such a plan. I call it the freedom plan.

Chapter 8

Satan's Freedom Plan

Satan's freedom plan is an enormous deception because it does not *create* freedom, it actually *destroys* it. Freedom requires that there be different results from choices. Having differences in the results is critical, because results determine whether a choice is good or bad and to what degree. How different the results are determines how different the choices are.

Consider the choice of your driving speed. What makes the choice to drive 5 mph over the limit different from driving 15 mph over or 50 mph over? It is the consequences. The consequences are different, whether you get caught or not.

The results of a choice determine the nature of the choice. *Choices are not different if the results are all the same.* If we received the same results from all of our choices, then it would not matter which choice we made.

Remember the part of the object lesson when I held my two hands out with a penny in each hand? The student was not really free to choose because the results of his choices were the same. It wouldn't have mattered what the penny represented; freedom was still destroyed. Suppose each penny represented hell. No matter which hand is chosen, hell would be the result, which would be unfair. Would this not also be true if each penny represented heaven? If heaven was the result of both choices, would we be any more free to choose? We still would not be free, though we may not know it, or may not care. The deception behind this condition is greater when we are receiving something we want. Herein is part of the genius in the freedom plan.

The False Freedom of Saving Men in Sin

There is more to agency than merely being free to choose, which is probably why, according to President J. Reuben Clark, there is more than one way to destroy it. He apparently pondered the dilemma about how Satan was going to destroy our agency and decided upon basically the same two possibilities we have discussed. "As I read the scriptures, *Satan's plan required one of two things*: Either the *compulsion* of the mind, the spirit, the intelligence of man, or else *saving men in sin*" (J. Reuben Clark, Jr., in Conference Report, Oct. 1949, 193; emphasis added).

President Clark saw the first possibility as "compulsion of the mind," which we have compared to the force plan. He then said there was a second possibility for Satan's plan, that of saving men *in* their sins, which we have called the freedom plan. Saving men *in* their sins means that men would be "free" to sin without penalty, receiving salvation despite unrighteousness. Saving men *in* their sins means that there would be no need for repentance. Saving all men regardless of their choices would effectively destroy men's agency, their stewardships, by not making them accountable for their choices.

In this way Lucifer cleverly changed the definition of freedom to "choice without penalty" instead of "choice without compulsion." He did so by proposing to redeem all mankind without any requirements on their part. He told us we would be free to do as we pleased on earth and in the end we would all be granted salvation regardless of what we did. This is basically the University of Freedom concept. It has the same benefits of guaranteed salvation as the force plan, but it is without the obvious negatives.

The Freedom Plan Limits Results Not Choices

The only appeal in the force plan was its guarantee of salvation. But wouldn't the same guarantee of salvation be far more appealing if it was given for free? Who would choose to be forced with a guarantee of salvation when they could do as they please and be guaranteed the same thing? According to George Q. Cannon, Satan's plan was to save everyone regardless of their choices. "The division occurred, as we are now informed, through a difference of views concerning the plan of salvation. Satan desired that man should be saved through the taking away from him of his agency. He would *save everybody regardless of their own acts*" (George Q. Cannon, *Collected Discourses*, Vol. 2, May 1891; emphasis added).

In order to "save everybody regardless of their own acts," they must first be free to act. This does not describe a plan to force everyone to be righteous; it describes a plan to give away salvation regardless of the choices people make.

Both the force plan and freedom plan would destroy agency. The force plan limits choices while the freedom plan limits results. What do the scriptures say about it? The only scripture that gives much detail of Satan's actual proposal is Moses 4:1. In this scripture, what is being limited, *choices or results*? "Satan . . . came before me saying—

Behold, here am I, send me, I will be thy son, and I will *redeem all mankind, that one soul shall not be lost,* and surely I will do it; wherefore give me thine honor" (Moses 4:1; emphasis added).

There is no mention of Satan attempting to limit our choices in this verse. He commits *himself* to doing something but makes no demands on us at all. The redemption of all mankind was something *Lucifer* offered to do, not something *we* could do. Since our redemption is a result, not a choice, the only thing being limited is the results of our choices. Just like in the University of Freedom, no demands were made on us. Since the scripture actually says that what is being limited is a result rather than a choice, the weight of evidence for Satan's proposal now shifts in favor of the freedom plan.

Satan—the Accuser and the Salesman

Satan is called "the accuser of our brethren" (Revelation 12:10), because that is what he does. But before he became "the accuser of our *brethren*," he was accusing the Father and the Son. Judging by the fact that he persuaded a "third part" to follow him (Revelation 12:4), we can safely imagine that he was a being of great charisma. No doubt he was very eloquent, articulate, and convincing. He has trained many anti-Christs like Sherem and Korihor who certainly were (Jacob 7:4; Alma 30:42, 53). They were like Zeezrom "who was expert in the devices of the devil" (Alma 11:21). Such people promote their agendas by flattering those who agree with them and accusing those who do not. People are easy to flatter, but Father is a perfect being, so what could Satan possibly accuse Father of?

The fact is, that people who strictly adhere to the rule of law are often targets of accusation.

Just as Korihor accused Alma of keeping his people in bondage,

Chapter 8 ~ Satan's Freedom Plan

Satan probably accused Father of something similar, and for similar reasons. Alma was enforcing divine laws by holding people accountable (Alma 30:9–11). God does the same thing (D&C 58:30–32). To Satan, this was the weakness in Father's plan, because it meant that not all would qualify to return to Father's presence and become like Him (D&C 132:20–23). With many falling short of exaltation, accusations of injustice and unfairness were easy to make. It would be easy to point out that we would be in a state of ignorance on earth, yet we would be expected to seek out the truth, find it, and strictly follow it. To qualify for salvation, we would have to do everything in Father's way and absolutely according to *His* laws and *His* will (D&C 105:5). This is precisely the kind of accountability that most people try to avoid.

In his sales pitch, Satan could have correctly argued that by the normal experiences of mortality, under his freedom plan everyone would still learn the principles of good and evil because the natural consequences of life would still apply. We would still have learned that all things have their opposites from virtue and vice to pleasure and pain. Since we would all experience the natural consequences of right and wrong, we would have learned our lessons, so he would claim that there would be no need for eternal penalty. This would be sufficient grounds on which to forgive everyone and grant salvation to all. This was Satan's freedom proposal— the freedom from failure and the freedom from punishment.

Satan's rebellion was a war fought on two fronts: (1) he accused the Father of lacking mercy and compassion and (2) he lured his followers with a flattering sales pitch of guaranteed salvation at no cost to them.

The Consequences of Having No Consequences

Under the freedom plan Satan's atonement offered unconditional mercy that would have virtually eliminated the possibility of failure. Though it sounds very compassionate, the truth is it would have "destroy[ed] the work of justice" and "if so, God would [have] cease[d] to be God" (Alma 42:13). This unconditional forgiveness would have violated the second element of agency—that the results of choices must be different.

The idea of unconditional salvation is as popular today as it ever has been. Satan has used this false hope to corrupt the minds of the natural man for centuries. Elder Dallin H. Oaks recognized this heresy as the plan of Satan: "The Zoramites worshiped a god . . . who had 'elected' them that they all would be saved (Alma 31:15–17). From this description it appears that the Zoramites were, knowingly or unknowingly, worshiping the person and *plan of Satan*" (Dallin H. Oaks, *Pure in Heart* [1988], 126; emphasis added).

The Zoramites were not being forced to be righteous, so how could they have been worshiping the plan of Satan if forcing us to be righteous was his plan? On the contrary, the Zoramites "would not observe to keep the commandments of God" and yet they believed they would still be saved (Alma 31:9, 16). When people think they will be saved regardless of what they do, their behavior deteriorates almost every time. So the consequence of believing there are no consequences is a life of misery, for "wickedness never was happiness" (Alma 41:10).

Chapter 8 ~ SATAN'S FREEDOM PLAN

Religious and Secular Popularity of The Freedom Plan

There is nothing fun about repentance, so the natural man prefers to avoid it. He prefers to make his own rules. But in Father's plan, with no repentance *from* sin we die *in* our sins. If we die *in* our sins, we cannot be saved *from* them. The Book of Mormon teaches this very plainly.

> And remember also the words which Amulek spake unto Zeezrom, in the city of Ammonihah; for he said unto him that the Lord surely should come to redeem his people, but that he should *not* come to redeem them *in* their sins, but to redeem them *from* their sins. And he hath power given unto him from the Father to redeem them *from* their sins because of repentance. [Helaman 5:10–11; emphasis added]

The people of Ammonihah were among the most wicked of all groups in the Book of Mormon. They burned alive the women and children of those who had been converted (Alma 14:8–10), then justified this horrible deed by claiming they "did not believe in the repentance of their sins" (Alma 15:15). They had abandoned all sense of accountability.

Many philosophies of men also embrace the freedom plan. Though they are not labeled as religious in nature, they are often adopted in response to religious principles, because they either minimize or eliminate the need for repentance. This is a very popular philosophy. The secular doctrines of the world grow from the heart of the natural man. Whether it be humanism, atheism, Darwinism or any other "ism," each has its roots embedded in a desire to avoid divine accountability.

This is exactly why Darwin's theory of spontaneous organic

evolution is so popular today. It conveniently encourages atheism, because if there is no God, then values are completely relative and we can decide right or wrong for ourselves. Believers in Darwinism can make their own rules and do as they please. There is no need to worry about consequences. Their logic says that if our ancestors crawled out of a swamp 500 million years ago then there is no God to answer to, and we are just highly developed animals. If so, then there are no standards of morality except those we create for ourselves. "They hearken not unto the counsel of God, for they set it aside, *supposing they know of themselves*" (2 Nephi 9:28; emphasis added). So it is that they spend all the days of their lives vainly seeking "happiness in doing iniquity" (Helaman 13:38).

The freedom plan appeals to the religious just as easily. In fact, every false doctrine taught by every anti-Christ in the Book of Mormon boils down to an attempt to avoid accountability. Most of the false beliefs in the man-made religions of the world are either based upon or influenced by this same desire to minimize or customize accountability. Instead of believing in a God that "cannot look upon sin with the least degree of allowance," "every man walketh in his own way, and after the image of his own god" (D&C 1:31, 16). The "eat, drink, and be merry" advocates are in this category:

> Yea, and there shall be many which shall say: Eat, drink, and be merry, for tomorrow we die; and it shall be well with us.
>
> And there shall also be many which shall say: Eat, drink, and be merry; *nevertheless, fear God—he will justify in committing a little sin*; yea, lie a little, take the advantage of one because of his words, dig a pit for thy neighbor; there is no harm in this; and do all these things, for tomorrow we die; *and if it so be that we are guilty, God will beat us with a few stripes, and at last we shall be saved* in the kingdom of God. [2 Nephi 28:7–8; emphasis added]

This group of believers doesn't *eliminate* accountability, but they do *reduce* it to their own comfort level. Almost all false doctrine customizes accountability in some way. By contrast, every true doctrine preserves the principle of individual accountability just as the scriptures describe it and as the Atonement demands it.

Grace and Accountability

Avoiding accountability is often the unspoken motive of those who profess to believe that works have nothing to do with salvation. If it is by grace alone that we are saved after nothing more than a sincere confession that Jesus is the Savior, then it is easy to "justify in committing a little sin" and believe that "at last we shall be saved in the kingdom of God" (2 Nephi 28:8). Under this philosophy, the doctrine of repentance, rather than being a requirement for salvation, is merely a sign of a good believer.

If repentance is not required, few believers will do much repenting because it is so difficult. Most will skip the tough part because they believe they are saved anyway. Why bother struggling to climb a mountain if someone offers to give you a free ride to the top? The grace only doctrine claims to save people *in* their sins, thus destroying accountability by withholding any penalty and granting an unconditional reward.

This "saved by grace" doctrine is not far from Satan's freedom plan. The major difference is that Satan proposed to save everyone, not just the believers. The major similarity is also the reason for its popularity: it reduces the level of accountability. But Jesus did not tell us to *wear* the cross; He told us to *carry* it (Luke 14:27).

The Freedom Plan Was an Attempt to Destroy Accountability

Accountability, or stewardship, was the principle which we fought to preserve in the War in Heaven, although scripture uses the word *agency* to describe it. The problem for us is that this war has come to earth and Satan's plan has not changed. It is not choice but agency that is once again under attack. His method is to get us to focus more on the enticements of our choices than on the results those choices can bring.

Considering the popularity of avoiding accountability today, it is a wonder that Father did not lose many more of His children in that premortal conflict. Satan's plan may well have appealed to more than "a third part," but people were only cast out for rebellion, not for just wanting another plan (D&C 29:36). The problem is that many others, such as Cain, probably liked the idea of choice without penalty (Moses 5:24), and they have come to earth with those same irresponsible attitudes.

To put an end to the premortal conflict, Father, rather than forfeit the principle of accountability, exercised it. He executed the penalty for rebellion, even though it cost Him "a third part" of His children (Revelation 12:4; D&C 29:36). Father is obviously very serious about preserving our stewardships by holding us accountable for our actions.

> What, do ye suppose that mercy can rob justice? I say unto you, Nay; not one whit. If so, God would cease to be God. [Alma 42:25]
>
> Who am I that made man, saith the Lord, that will hold him guiltless that obeys not my commandments?
>
> Who am I, saith the Lord, that have promised and have not fulfilled?

Chapter 8 ~ SATAN'S FREEDOM PLAN

I command and men obey not; I revoke and they receive not the blessing. [D&C 58:30–32]

It is required of the Lord, at the hand of every steward, to render an account of his stewardship, both in time and in eternity. [D&C 72:3]

The remainder of this book will show examples of how Satan has used the freedom plan throughout history including to our day. We will see that Satan taught the Gadianton robbers the tricks of the freedom plan. It was one of the secrets of their successful takeover of the Nephite government. It will then come as no surprise that these same tactics and methods are used by our modern day Gadiantons who also seek for power. Then in the final chapter we will consider how these same methods and principles apply to the way we teach our children and the results they bring into our children's lives.

Chapter 9

The Gadiantons Used the Freedom Plan

The Incredible Success of the Gadiantons

The Book of Mormon tells a sad story of a people called the Nephites who often bled and died in battle, determined to preserve their freedom only to trade it away in the end. In exchange, they got nothing but "fair promises" from an organized gang of traitors called the Gadianton robbers (Ether 8:17). The group got started when a man named Gadianton organized a gang of assassins who were united by a secret oath to help and defend each other (Helaman 2:1–5). This organization was so effective that in only 26 years the Gadiantons succeeded in doing what the Lamanite armies had not been able to do in half a millennia. "They did obtain the sole management of the government" (Helaman 6:39).

For some 500 years the Lamanites had attempted to enslave the Nephites by attacking with their armies. Although the Nephites were always greatly outnumbered, the faithful were never brought into bondage by force of arms. The cause of freedom burned so strongly within them that they gave up their lives by the thousands to "preserve their rights and their privileges, yea, and also their liberty" (Alma 43:9). Direct attempts to take away freedom are like the force plan and are always strongly opposed. Observing that the Lamanite's force plan approach had always failed, the Gadiantons used the freedom plan instead.

The Gadiantons worked mostly from the inside. They were so effective that the Nephites were not only *unaware* that they were losing their freedom, they were not even aware when it was gone. In fact, by the time the Gadiantons "did obtain the sole management of the government" (Helaman 6:39), the Nephites actually thought they were more free than they had ever been. What kind of brilliant scheme could convince people that they are gaining more and more of the very thing they continue to lose? It is the ultimate scam, Satan's freedom plan.

The secret to the Gadianton's success was identified by Joseph Smith. As John Taylor recalled:

> These secret combinations were spoken of by Joseph Smith, years and years ago. I have heard him time and time again tell about them, and he stated that when these things began to take place the liberties of this nation would begin to be *bartered away* (John Taylor in *Journal of Discourses* [1882], 22:143; emphasis added).

The reason the freedom plan works so well is that in order to destroy people's freedom, you do not have to steal it from them. You only need to barter with them until they trade it away. In effect, the deal is, "I'll give you what you want if you give me what I want." It is an offer that many cannot refuse. It also parallels the strategy of the freedom plan Satan used in the War in Heaven.

Chapter 9 ~ The Gadiantons Used the Freedom Plan

What Is a "Secret Combination?"

The Book of Mormon called the organization a secret combination, which does not mean it was some kind of secret code (though the Gadiantons did use such things). A secret combination is when people "*unite*" and "enter into a covenant one with another . . . to *combine* against all righteousness" (3 Nephi 6:27–28; emphasis added). By this definition, whenever two or more people secretly unite in doing evil, they have formed a secret combination. Needless to say, secret combinations are found almost everywhere at every level of society. The Gadiantons were only the highest level of it, or the lowest, depending on how you look at it. They are the ones who, like Satan, sought to obtain power over a free people.

The record states that the Gadiantons made oaths with each other "to help such as sought power to gain power and to successfully murder, and to plunder, and to lie, and to commit all manner of wickedness and whoredoms" (Ether 8:16). In short, they had a dual purpose: (1) to obtain power and (2) to get away with sin. The deal they made with the Nephites was, "if you give us power, we will let you get away with sin."

Corrupt People are the Key to Success

The Nephite democracy was *not* the Gadianton's greatest obstacle. In fact, the Nephite elections actually made it easier for the Gadiantons. When kings reigned, obtaining the throne required conquering the king's army and establishing a new dynasty. This was no easy task, as the Lamanites could testify. But to obtain power under the reign of the judges, all the Gadiantons had to do was get elected. They did get elected too, because "the Nephites did build them [the Gadiantons] up and support them . . . until they had overspread all the land of the Nephites" (Helaman 6:38). But why would the Nephites, who had a democracy, willingly vote for people who sought "to overthrow the freedom of all lands, nations, and countries" (Ether 8:25)? And why would a righteous people like the Nephites elect wicked men who wanted to "murder, and to plunder, and to lie, and to commit all manner of wickedness and whoredoms" (Ether 8:16)? They wouldn't, unless one of two things happened: (1) the Nephites *didn't know* the men were that wicked or (2) they *didn't care*.

To make sure the Nephites did not know the truth, the Gadianton organizations were always secretive. Secrecy was necessary "to keep them in darkness" (Ether 8:16). It is the glue that holds Satan's kingdom together. But ultimately, getting the Nephites to not care was the higher priority, because then, even if someone got caught doing wrong, they could still avoid penalty because no one cared enough to do anything about it. But there was another advantage for the Gadiantons. People who do not care about iniquity actually support it by not opposing it. In short, the reason the Nephites did not care what the Gadiantons were doing is that the Gadiantons let them do the same things.

So the first objective was to corrupt the people that they might be more supportive of the Gadianton cause and agenda. The method of corruption was seduction, telling the people what they wanted to hear. The record says the Gadiantons "had *seduced* the more part of the righteous until they had come down to believe in their works and partake of their spoils, and to join with them in their secret murders and combinations" (Helaman 6:38; emphasis added). The people were seduced into thinking that they were free to sin and avoid accountability. This approach had the same objectives and destroyed agency in basically the same way as did Satan's freedom plan.

Chapter 9   The Gadiantons Used the Freedom Plan

The Source of Gadianton Doctrine

You may recall that the anti-Christ Korihor was very good at seduction. He taught a philosophy which justified adultery and sought to have its status changed from a crime to a sin, thereby avoiding civil accountability for it (Alma 30:10, 18). It was a popular theme and made a great campaign issue.

Though it is clear that the Gadiantons taught Korihor's doctrine, we can not blame Korihor alone for infecting them with it. Mormon explained that "those secret oaths and covenants . . . were put into the heart of Gadianton by that same being who did entice our first parents" (Helaman 6:26). Korihor was taught by Satan. He admitted this, saying, "the devil hath deceived me; for he appeared unto me in the form of an angel . . . and he taught me that which I should say" (Alma 30:53). The doctrine of the anti-Christs and the Gadiantons is the doctrine of Satan. It seduces people by flattering them into believing they can avoid the consequences of sin. The use of flattery by anti-Christs and Gadiantons is well documented (Jacob 7:4; Alma 30:47; 61:4; Helaman 2:5; 3 Nephi 1:29; Ether 8:2) It is the same old freedom plan.

Corrupting the Legal System

One of the main obstacles for the Gadiantons was the Nephite legal system. The righteous king Mosiah said the Nephite laws were "correct, and . . . were given them by the hand of the Lord" (Mosiah 29:25). The Nephite laws imposed penalties for crime *and even for some sins*. So the Gadiantons had to change this if they were going to get away with crime and sin. They worked mostly from inside the institutions of society, but on two fronts: (1) charismatic Korihor types worked on corrupting the morals of the people, while (2) lawyers and civil officials worked on corrupting the laws. Each objective benefitted the other, for corrupt laws corrupt people, and corrupt people corrupt laws (Helaman 4:22–24; 5:2–3).

It only took twenty years before "their laws had become corrupted" because "they had altered . . . the laws" (Helaman 4:22). The lawyers and officials may have rewritten the laws, but it was the people themselves who allowed their laws to become corrupted.

> For as their laws and their governments were established by the voice of the people, and they who chose evil were more numerous than they who chose good, therefore they were ripening for destruction, for the laws had become corrupted. Yea, and this was not all; they were a stiffnecked people, insomuch that they could not be governed by the law nor justice, save it were to their destruction. [Helaman 5:2–3]

How do people corrupt divine laws? They simply change them. Any alteration of a divine law without instruction from the divine is a corruption of the law. So whether you believe Satan used the force or freedom plan, the corruption of divine law is exactly what he tried to do in the War in Heaven. He did so for the same reasons and by the same method as the Gadiantons—to gain power by the use of flattery.

"Fair Promises" Bring Protection and Election

The Gadiantons recruited their members with a seductive flattery of "fair promises" (Ether 8:17). It enticed the Nephites to "unite with those bands of robbers." The main promise was "that they would protect and preserve one another in whatsoever difficult circumstances they should be placed, *that they should not suffer* for their murders, and their plunderings, and their stealings" (Helaman 6:21; emphasis added). By this means the Gadiantons "*seduced* the more

Chapter 9   ∽   The Gadiantons Used the Freedom Plan

part of the righteous until they had come down to believe in their works and partake of their spoils, and to join with them in their secret murders and combinations" (Helaman 6:38; emphasis added).

This promise of protection among the Gadianton brotherhood assured that fellow members would not be prosecuted for committing crimes. When people joined the secret society, they were able to do as they pleased because the society would close ranks to protect them. In this way they helped each other avoid accountability. The reason why political power is always the goal is that enforcement of the law is always in the hands of those who administer it. Once the Gadiantons obtained the key positions, a man charged with a crime could be set free by his brothers in the judgement seats.

When the Nephites were righteous, the Gadiantons had a hard time getting elected because "the voice of the people" usually came in favor of the more righteous candidates (Mosiah 29:26; 3 Nephi 3:19). This presented a problem for the Gadiantons, so their efforts were primarily to deceive the Nephites by pretending to be righteous and by influencing more people to become wicked like themselves.

The Gadiantons accomplished both these objectives by preaching the doctrine of the freedom plan. They pretended to have a higher morality and a greater sense of justice than their opponents (Mosiah 10:12–13; Alma 54:17; 3 Nephi 3:5). This included making accusations against those who would not compromise their principles or adapt to the times. They also promised the people that if given the power, they would expand their freedoms and rights by minimizing or eliminating the penalties for certain sins they wanted to commit (Alma 30:17–18; 3 Nephi 3:6–10).

Their success requires getting elected, but generally only the wicked knowingly vote for the wicked. For Gadiantons to get the votes, social norms have to decline. Legalizing sin is only the first phase of this process. With time and effort, the spiritual poison of unaccountability can be administered "by degrees" (Alma 47:18). Corrupt politicians change the status of sin from illegal to unpunishable, and then to legal. The people themselves do the rest. Legal sin evolves from permissible to acceptable, and then to normal. From there it becomes preferable and even mandatory as people become ripe for destruction (Genesis 19:4–9).

Thus the enticing promise of protection goes beyond protection against civil penalty; it includes protection against social stigma. This is accomplished by increasing the proportion of wicked people in a society. As more people become wicked, they effectively become supporters of the Gadiantons. They do not have to actually join them by taking a secret oath. They only need to consent to the changes and sustain those who make them until those who choose evil outnumber those who choose good (Helaman 5:2).

The Surrender to Seduction

The invitation to join the Gadianton collective was never more clear than when Giddianhi, the governor of the Gadianton band, wrote a letter to Lachoneus, the governor of the righteous, saying; "Yield yourselves up unto us, and unite with us and become acquainted with our secret works, and become our brethren that ye may be like unto us—not our slaves, but our brethren and partners of all our substance" (3 Nephi 3:7). This kind of invitation successfully lured many thousands of Nephites and Lamanites to join the Gadiantons over the years. But it was this offer of protection from accountability that made it possible for the Gadiantons to obtain "sole management of the government" (Helaman 6:39).

Once it became well established, a multi-layered symbiotic relationship existed in their society. The Gadiantons depended upon the people's votes to keep them in office and the people depended on

Chapter 9 ~ THE GADIANTONS USED THE FREEDOM PLAN

the Gadiantons to keep altering the laws to make more sins legal. The more people joined the collective, the greater the protection for everyone, resulting in even greater wickedness.

In the end the Gadiantons did not have to *take* control of the government because the Nephites *gave* it to them. Like Satan, they seduced the people with fair promises from corrupt politicians who were not really interested in preserving rights or freedom. So what one generation of Nephites had bled and died to preserve, the next generation willingly gave away. They simply surrendered to the Gadiantons without a fight. Like the third of the hosts of heaven, the Nephites surrendered to seduction, actually joining in the rebellion and supporting those who sought power over them.

And thus we see that the desire to escape accountability is the reason why "the Nephites did build them up and support them." It is also why this doctrine was first successful among "the more wicked part" of the Nephite society (Helaman 6:38). The righteous are not as easily deceived because they accept their accountability and understand it to be essential to their freedom. In the Nephite's golden years they who chose good were more numerous than they who chose evil, so the wicked had a hard time getting elected (3 Nephi 3:19). This is why it was not possible for the Gadiantons to gain political power until after they "had seduced the more part of the righteous until they had come down to believe in their works and partake of their spoils" (Helaman 6:38). Having flattered the wicked and seduced the righteous, the Gadiantons were assured election, because those who still embraced the principle of accountability became the minority.

The Symbiotic Relationship Turned Parasitic

The Gadiantons got what they wanted by giving the people what they wanted, but because this symbiotic relationship was purely selfish, it was doomed to fail. The desires of both sides could never have made either of them happy, for they "sought all the days of [their] lives for that which [they] could not obtain." They "sought for happiness in doing iniquity" (Helaman 13:38).

The wicked do not *serve* each other, they *use* each other, so their symbiotic relationship was really only an illusion. Both sides were actually parasites, feeding upon each other's resources. The Gadiantons syphoned the people's wealth, absorbed their votes, and devoured their government. The people were feasting off their benefactor's promises to let them do as they pleased. The unsolvable problem for the Gadiantons was that power is an insatiable lust, a desire that cannot be satisfied. No matter how much power they attained, it was never enough. The unsolvable problem for the people was that unleashed iniquity is also an insatiable lust. They could not commit enough iniquity to satisfy their starving souls, for "there is no peace, saith the Lord, unto the wicked" (Isaiah 48:22).

Once a people "lift up their heads in their wickedness" (Alma 30:18) and glory in it as Cain did (Moses 5:31), their moral decay is very rapid. Destruction is the only possible outcome for a nation terminally infected with this disease (Ether 8:22). Parasites, if not stopped, will eventually destroy their host. When the Gadianton sickness had finally killed the host society that had always fed them, the people quickly turned on each other. The Lord didn't have to destroy them; they destroyed themselves.

The "do as you please" doctrine of the freedom plan was as pop-

Chapter 9 — THE GADIANTONS USED THE FREEDOM PLAN

ular as ever among the Nephites. Not worrying about consequences was the bait that lured them into supporting the wicked who sought for power. As soon as the people accepted the idea that they were not accountable for sin, the erosion of their freedom began. Limiting their consequences limited their freedom long before the Gadiantons obtained the government. If it weren't for the freedom plan, the secret combinations could not have survived. Is it really any different today?

Chapter 10

Modern Gadiantons

They aren't known as Gadiantons anymore, but those who seek to corrupt society are just as secret and just as dangerous (Ether 8:20–25). Like their ancient counterparts, they still want power, still seek to avoid accountability, still seek to corrupt the population, and still use the freedom plan. Their methods are also much the same, of which there are far too many to mention here. Only two of their tools will be exposed: (1) money and (2) flattery. With these two they obtain much of their popularity.

President Ezra Taft Benson noticed the similarity between the methods used by today's power seekers and those used during the War in Heaven. "'You want to be loved by everyone,' says the devil, 'and this *freedom battle* is so controversial you might be accused of engaging in politics.' . . . Some might even call the War in Heaven a political struggle—certainly it was controversial" (Ezra Taft Benson, *The Teachings of Ezra Taft Benson* [1988], 659; emphasis added). I will not mention any names or political parties because I do not wish to be "engaging in politics." For the record, although I do not believe every politician is corrupt, I do believe that some degree of Gadiantonism can be found in every political party. My purpose here is to expose only two methods of the modern Gadiantons so that you can recognize them wherever they exist. You can attach the labels yourself.

A Hand Up or a Hand Out?

Political success depends on popularity. What better way is there to become popular than by giving away money? It is a very old practice. An ancient Jaredite secret combination once sought to overthrow their father's kingdom. They seduced enough people to divide the kingdom, start a civil war and destroy almost everyone in the process. How they became popular was simple: "The sons of Akish did *offer them money,* by which means they drew away the more part of the people after them" (Ether 9:11; emphasis added).

Money is still a favorite bait with which modern Gadiantons lure their prey. Often only after the hook is set do people discover that the strings attached to their money are limiting their freedom. President Benson said:

> Today the devil as a wolf in a supposedly new suit of sheep's clothing is enticing some men, both in and out of the Church, to parrot his line by advocating planned government-guaranteed security programs at the expense of our liberties. Latter-day Saints should be reminded how and why they voted as they did in heaven. If some have decided to change their vote they should repent—throw their support on the side of freedom—and cease promoting this subversion. [Ezra Taft Benson, Conference Report, Oct. 1961, 71]

President Benson compared today's guaranteed security programs to Lucifer's offer of guaranteed salvation, saying they were subversive to freedom. Of course, not all governmental assistance programs are subversive to freedom. The key to knowing the difference is understanding the relationship between dependence and independence, and the difference between a hand up and a handout.

Scriptures teach us that we have a moral obligation to care for the needy for as long as they are in need (Mosiah 2:16–23). But there is a difference between helping the incapable with a hand up, and supporting the lazy with endless handouts.

The Apostle Paul taught that "if any would not work, neither should he eat" (2 Thessalonians 3:10). Jesus practiced this principle after feeding the 5,000 (John 6:5–13). The day after this miracle of the free lunch, the people found Jesus again. Their motives for seeking Him, however, were not pure. He told them that they had sought Him not because they desired to follow His teachings but because they wanted another free meal (JST, John 6:26). Although Jesus was completely compassionate, He refused to feed them again. He knew that refusing them would cost Him popularity, and it did. As a result, "from that time many of his disciples went back, and walked no more with him" (John 6:66). Jesus never used the pretense of compassion to sacrifice accountability for popularity. But what would Satan have done?

Why do we call it compassion when assistance is given where it is not needed? Should wheelchairs be given to people who can walk, or hearing aids to people who can hear? Is this compassion? If these acts are not motivated by compassion, then by what are they motivated? If the motive is not service, then it must be selfishness.

True charity does not destroy accountability. A temporary hand up is given with the understanding that individual responsibility will be maintained. But Gadiantons prefer handouts because they are popular, and popularity brings power, which in turn enables control.

Dependence Is Not Independence

Some people do not mind government control as long as they are pacified with support from the public treasury. For them, the government becomes the nursing mother. The problem is that instead of eventually weaning the child, this mother addicts the child to her constant nourishment. Both mother and child get what they want: the child does not have to work for a living, and the mother stays in complete control of the child's life. President Benson stated:

> This freedom must be continually guarded as something more priceless than life itself. Any program that would tend to weaken this freedom is inherently dangerous and should be guarded against . . . this philosophy of individual freedom and citizenship responsibility, based upon the principle of helping the individual to help himself, and discouraging people from expecting the government to support them, but encouraging them to support their own government. [Ezra Taft Benson, Conference Report, April 1953, 40]

Dependence and independence are inversely proportional. With too much independence we do not have a nation, but with too much dependence we lose our freedom. The right balance must be maintained. Remember, Lucifer's offer of universal salvation not only made us completely dependent upon him, but required nothing of us. By this means we would have lost our independence, because no matter what we did, there would only have been one result. Under the freedom plan we would have had no responsibility at all; we could not have failed. Likewise, the more the government imitates the freedom plan, the tighter its grip becomes.

A well-balanced interdependence between a people and their government creates a mutual accountability. Consider the teenage boy who wants freedom from his parents. He wants to move out and live on his own, but he has no education, no job, and no money. He cannot be free because he is completely dependent upon his parents for financial support.

Hollywood Gadiantons

Obviously not all Gadiantons are in the government. Most in fact are not. Government Gadiantons do their part to corrupt the laws, but they do not really corrupt the people. The people do that themselves. Since corruption precedes seduction, the corruption of the people is a high priority for Gadiantons. The two biggest problems for them are the positive influences of family and religion, but even these enormous obstacles can be overcome by carefully shifting people's allegiance away from their family and religion. This is where Hollywood and others among the rich and famous come in. They employ charismatic Korihors whose first mission is to become more popular than either family or religion. The corruption begins as the people look to these popular Korihors not only for their entertainment, but also for their standards of morality. This effort requires that the Korihors persist and insist that they are the moral standards of the civilization. They win our *affection* by entertaining us so well that the real world appears boring. To win our *allegiance* they must do much more. For this job, they need a special tool.

Flattering People with a New Vocabulary

When the wicked use flattery there is always a well-hidden agenda beneath the rhetoric: to convince people of their higher morality, greater sensitivity and superior compassion. Part of today's strategy to lead society into a new morality has been to create a new vocabulary. Society itself can be moved in one direction or another simply by adopting or forbidding the use of certain words.

This flattering new language is called "political correctness." Its name is designed so that it tolerates no questions about its morality. Those who use it out of a sincere desire to be respectful and sensitive are *not* the problem; those who have a subversive agenda in mind when creating it, promoting it and insisting upon its use *are* the problem.

Lucifer used his own kind of political correctness in the War in Heaven. He changed the meaning of freedom from "choice without compulsion" to "choice without penalty." He also redefined what it meant to be loving, caring, and compassionate. He pretended to be on the "moral high ground" by promising salvation to every soul. Thus his definition of generosity, compassion and love meant letting us do as we please, while those who opposed him were accused of being "mean spirited" and "divisive."

Like the Pharisees of old, today's Gadiantons, using their flattering new words, often "outwardly appear righteous unto men, but within . . . are full of hypocrisy and iniquity" (Matthew 23:28). By labeling this new language "correct," they have assured that anyone not using it can be labeled "incorrect." The deception is that if we assume the *words* are morally correct, then the *philosophy* behind them must be correct as well. This is the exact purpose of such language.

Some of these modern-day Pharisees love to set traps for those they wish to accuse. In order to "make a man an offender for a word" (Isaiah 29:21), they first decide what words are appropriate, acceptable and "correct," then "watch for iniquity" until someone slips (v. 20). At that point they spring the trap and make the accusation in order to make themselves appear morally superior to their opponents, whom they accuse of being "bigoted," "mean spirited," or "insensitive." So in the end, it is often those who are the loudest in demanding tolerance who have the least tolerance for those who disagree with them.

Some "Politically Correct" Examples

Political correctness can certainly be a tool for positive change, but it all depends on the motives of those using it. Many of the changes in definitions have a hidden agenda behind their subtle message. The message is often, Do as you please, and don't worry about the consequences." The hidden agenda is the power or popularity the user seeks to attain.

For example, Hollywood Korihors sell violence to our children but are careful to call it "action." Script writers require young actors to use all kinds of vulgarity and sexual language because this is "normal." They justify almost every abominable thing in the name of "entertainment." Thus while Hollywood pretends to be *reflecting* the norms of society, they are instead attempting to *create* them. If "by their fruits ye shall know them" (Matthew 7:20), then their agenda is in their scripts!

Government Gadiantons make their own contribution. They call exploiting the poor a "lottery." Gambling is called "gaming." Rewarding laziness is called "welfare." Abusing power is just "political skill." Voting against their agenda is "partisan," but their voting against your's is "ethical." They never get angry, only "upset" or "concerned," but your anger is a sign of "meanness." They oppose your agenda out of "political strategy." When you oppose their agenda, you are "divisive." Jesus called people like this "scribes and Pharisees, hypocrites . . . which strain at a gnat and swallow a camel" (Matthew 23:23–24).

Many schools do it too. Advancing students regardless of performance is called "building self-esteem." Discipline was first labeled as "archaic" and then "abusive." Eliminating discipline is called "progressive education." The resulting rebellion is passed off as "individuality." Defiance is excused as "free expression." Abandonment of traditional values is called "innovation." Scoffing at morality is "enlightenment," while holding to those values is "narrow minded." Biblical creation is a "myth," whereas spontaneous evolution is called a "fact."

Even the most fundamental values can be twisted by a "politically correct" definition. "Love" used to be a selfless caring emotion, but now it is a selfish sexual passion. Nowadays, adultery is only an "affair." Young people do not commit fornication anymore, they're just "sexually active." Whores became known as "prostitutes" but are now "sex workers," "call girls," or even "service women." Perversion is nothing more than an "alternative lifestyle." I have even heard bestiality justified by someone who said he was "open minded" about it. But who can be surprised at this, when an unborn child is only a "fetus," and killing it is only a "right" or a "choice?" These things are but echos from the past. Anciently, many like Korihor caused people "to lift up their heads in their wickedness . . . leading away many women, and also men, to commit whoredoms" (Alma 30:18).

By allowing these self-proclaimed moralists to establish the standards of acceptable *speech*, we eventually allow them to set the standards of *morality*. The shift is so subtle that most people do not even notice that their allegiance is shifting from God to man—something Nephi warned us about: "For I know that cursed is he that putteth his trust in the arm of flesh. Yea, cursed is he that putteth his trust in man or maketh flesh his arm" (2 Nephi 4:34).

The War in Heaven Brought to Earth

The War in Heaven has come to earth and the battle for the minds of men is still raging. Satan has many armies assigned to various missions. Hollywood advertises the doctrine of Korihor and sells it to the eager masses, "causing them to lift up their heads in their wickedness, yea, leading away many women, and also men, to commit whoredoms" (Alma 30:18). Scientists provide justification for fornication, "telling them that when a man [is] dead, that [is] the end thereof" (v. 18). Politicians clear the way, corrupting laws by legalizing sin. Thus under the camouflage of protecting rights, the *wrong* rights are granted, giving preference to the nonreligious. As freedoms begin to erode, financial prosperity provides sufficient money for the Gadianton leeches to bleed the system without killing it and enough distraction so that few people notice or care about the growing cancer. In this way the people are "seduced" until "the more part of the righteousness . . . come down to believe in their works and partake of their spoils" (Helaman 6:38).

Gadiantons continue Satan's war on agency in a variety of ways. The bribery of the lazy brings popularity. The flattery of political correctness provides a cloak of hypocritical righteousness, encourages the corruption of moral standards, and provides protection from correction. The corruption of good laws makes sin legal. Definitions of good and evil are reversed by granting the wrong set of rights. Fair promises of escaping accountability encourage expanding wickedness, which brings the popularity essential to draw the votes the Gadiantons need to "obtain the sole management of the government" (Helaman 6:39).

The most effective countermeasure in this war against the erosion of accountability is the influence of the family. No other institution can adequately replace the family because responsibility is best taught at home. This is exactly why Satan relentlessly attacks the family with every weapon available to him. Can you guess what his favorite strategy might be? It is none other than the freedom plan.

It is possible to compare these same methods and false principles of the freedom plan to those being practiced in Latter-day Saint homes today. What ancient Gadiantons *knowingly* did to destroy freedom, modern parents *unknowingly* do, but it is still the same old freedom plan. The incredible irony is that in their efforts to avoid what they thought was Satan's plan, many Latter-day Saint parents actually end up practicing and promoting it. Years later they sadly wonder why their children rebelled against the truth. After all, the freedom plan was what stirred up rebellion in the pre-earth life. Why wouldn't it be the cause of much of the rebellion today?

Chapter 11

Satan's War on the Family

The Perfect Parent

Now, "let us reason together, that ye may understand" (D&C 50:10). Since God is perfect and God is a parent, then God is a perfect parent. And since He wants us to become like Him (Leviticus 11:44–45), does it not stand to reason that He wants us to treat our children basically the same way He treats His? Since eternal parenthood is the ultimate measure of exaltation, can we not consider our stewardships as parents to be among the most important (D&C 132:20–22)? If having eternal posterity is the ultimate measure of exaltation, then many correct principles within the gospel must surely apply to parenting.

As a young convert, I learned from teachers that the gospel contained true principles by which we can govern every dimension of our lives. But as a young father, I went in search of true principles by which to raise my children, and I was repeatedly told that there were no true principles of parenting; that every parent had to figure it out for themselves; that what worked for one child might not work for the next. The common joke was that kids don't come with a manual.

There were plenty of books on parenting techniques, but I found no one who dared to suggest that there were true principles of parenting that applied to all cases. But why should differences in children mean that there cannot be true principles of parenting? If God is a perfect parent, then wouldn't He practice true principles of parenting, and couldn't we learn from Him?

Trying to emulate God in our parenting efforts does not promise to make it easy or guarantee success, but at least it shows us the right way. Since scriptures are the main source for obtaining knowledge of God's parenting skills (John 5:39), children, then, actually do come with a manual: the scriptures. Almost every page of scripture contains examples of how God teaches *His* children. When we "liken all scriptures unto us" (1 Nephi 19:23), searching the scriptures becomes a treasure hunt, only we find treasures *every* time we hunt. Reading the scriptures with this in mind can change our entire perspective about our relationship with our children. It can affect us, our children, and our children's children for generations to come.

Applying God's Principles Appropriately

The first step to finding true principles of parenting in the scriptures is to ask questions while we read. We can ask how God deals with His children in various situations. For example, how did God deal with Cain before the murder and after? If God loves His children, why did He allow Job to suffer so much? What attributes does God have that influence His children the most? Does He really treat each child equally? Does He use the same principles and methods with every child? If not, why not? Is God always kind, merciful, and generous? Do His children always respond positively to His efforts? What does God do when His children ignore, defy, or disobey Him? Does God ever get mad at His children? Does He ever raise His voice or punish His children? Under what conditions and how severely does He punish? Does punishment always work? All of these questions have a direct application to our own parenting efforts.

As answers begin to come, the next step is to appropriately apply these principles to ourselves and our children. However, it is important to keep in mind that not everything God does with His children is right for us to do with ours. God has the right to send His children into the spirit world, but we of course, do not. We should keep in mind that we are not looking for *methods* as much as for *principles*. Here, we can only focus on a few of the most fundamental principles that pertain to agency.

The Main Problem

A doctor always diagnoses a problem before prescribing a cure. So before we start looking for parenting solutions, it is best to identify the main problem. The main parenting problem is the influence of Satan. Satan's main method of bringing people to misery is the same as it always was, destroying the agency of man. He destroys agency the same way he did in the beginning, by using the freedom plan. He especially targets children because they are the most gullible, and he even uses parents to do the work for him.

All he has to do is get parents to limit the results of our children's choices. We usually do this in two ways: (1) we protect our children from failure and (2) we withhold penalty. To do either is to reward negative behavior. Doing so eliminates different results from different choices. Children who do not experience negative results for negative behavior grow up thinking life is like the University of Freedom and they can do as they please and never have to face unpleasant consequences. Parents who practice this philosophy may not realize that they are teaching their children the exact opposite of what they want them to learn.

This permissive practice is in direct conflict with one of the most fundamental purposes of life—to learn by experience the good from the evil. What does it mean to learn by experience if not to learn from the consequences of our decisions? The Lord explained this principle to our father Adam. Speaking of Adam's children, He said: "when they begin to grow up, sin conceiveth in their hearts, and they taste the bitter, that they may know to prize the good, (Moses 6:55). The Lord said that children learn to prize the good by tasting the bitter. How then can our children learn to prize the good if we do not allow them to taste the bitter? If we protect our children from the bitterness of their wrong choices, we deprive them of the moral foundation upon which they learn "to prize the good." Rebellious children have not learned to prize the good because they have not tasted enough bitterness to motivate them to change.

Thus Satan and permissive parents *both* promote the standards of the University of Freedom, but they have opposite motives and intent. Remember that Satan offered a condition in which everyone could do as they please and have no fear of failure or penalty. Parents do the same thing by protecting their children from failure and refusing to impose penalties. So *what Satan does by willful intent, parents may do by an honest mistake. Unfortunately, the effects of removing failure and penalty are the same, regardless of the intent.* Children from these homes have great difficulty using their agency wisely. These are the children we call rebellious. They are only rebellious because they have not learned to be responsible. But *children will never learn to be responsible until they are held responsible*. Not holding people responsible is what Satan's freedom plan is all about. The freedom plan offers love without law.

Love Without Law

God uses both love and law to influence his children. By "love,"

Chapter 11 — SATAN'S WAR ON THE FAMILY

I mean the *actions* of love which communicate the *emotion* of love. By "law," I mean all of those actions which involve establishing and enforcing the rules. What some parents forget is that it takes more than love to establish and build positive relationships. Remember that since all things are governed by law (D&C 88:34–38), loving relationships require law as well as love. You cannot have love without law.

It is hard to say whether love or law is the higher priority. With God it does not seem to matter, because both are always in effect in one way or another. The entire plan of salvation is given to us *because* of Father's *love* (John 3:16), and *through* His *laws* (D&C 132:11–12). His *law* is the means to attaining His *love* (1 Nephi 11:25), and His *love* is the reward for obeying His *law* (1 Nephi 11:21–23). Jesus said, "If ye *love* me, keep my *commandments*" (John 14:15), and "He that hath my *commandments*, and keepeth them . . . shall be *loved* of my Father, and I will *love* him" (John 14:21). Regardless of which is most important, *both* are essential to celestial relationships. When our children are born they are not capable of receiving or understanding law, but they respond very well to our love. We have an opportunity to show them love months before they begin to understand anything about law. This gives us an advantage, because when it comes time to teach and enforce the law, our love should not be in question. But if we wait until they are eight years old to start teaching them about law and accountability, we have waited far too long. They become accountable to *God* at age eight (D&C 29:47), but they are accountable to their *parents* as soon as they begin to understand instructions.

The focus here will be on law, *not* because love is unimportant, but because love is not usually what is missing. *Love is not the answer if love is not the question.* So contrary to some of our psychological dieticians, not every child suffers from a love deficiency, and not every child will be cured with nothing more than a higher dose of love. If a doctor diagnoses an infection, will he then treat for a broken bone? Even so, love is the cure *only* when love is the deficiency. The cause of the sickness among most of our wayward youth is not a lack of love but a lack of law.

When God gives His children law, all of the elements of agency are present. He tells us the rules which provide us with multiple choices. Then He attaches pleasant and unpleasant consequences to the choices. He creates freedom by giving us the ability to succeed or fail. He then informs us of the differences in the consequences. This makes us accountable for the consequences of our decisions. Finally, He delivers the promised consequence of the choice we make. The obedient choice brings blessings (D&C 130:20–21). For the disobedient, God "executeth the law, and the law inflicteth the punishment" (Alma 42:22).

All of these elements need to be present for agency to exist. To eliminate any one of them will "destroy the agency of man" (Moses 4:3). From the above list of requirements, what is generally missing from the lives of our rebellious youth? They have plenty of choices with different results. They are often even told of different consequences attached to their choices. What is usually missing is the delivery of different consequences.

When There's Law at Home

Both love and law need to be present in our homes. If either one is absent, then a divine principle is missing and divine blessings will be forfeited. A "law without love" home is like the military; there are plenty of rules and penalties, but there is no loving relationship. It is justice without mercy. It is a "do as I say or else" environment. The children of these homes often withdraw, respond with resentment, or eventually seek escape.

On the other hand, in a "love without law" home there is plenty of positive reinforcement, kindness, tenderness, and patience, but there are either no rules or no enforcement of rules. Usually the situation is one of rules without enforcement, but it amounts to the same thing as having no rules, for "how could there be a law save there was a punishment" (Alma 42:17). A "love without law" home is one in which mercy robs justice (v. 25). Many are under the illusion that *teaching* our children only requires *telling* them right from wrong. Some then believe that after having presented the choices clearly and having explained the natural or eternal consequences of each, our job as parents is basically done and any further involvement in the process is to interfere with agency. *Some parents reason that Satan wanted to force us to be righteous, so they equate enforcement with force. Based on these two false assumptions, they minimize or eliminate penalties for disobedience. So in an effort to avoid Satan's plan, they actually promote it.* While trying to avoid Force College, we sometimes create the University of Freedom instead. The philosophies of men reinforce this practice, but if we look closely, we see that God does not eliminate penalty and He forbids our doing so (Mosiah 4:14–15; D&C 1:31; 42:88–93; 64:12–13).

Without penalty, home becomes the same as the University of Freedom. To create a University of Freedom at home we can (1) simply let children do as they please and have no rules or (2) have rules, but not enforce them, in effect, permitting disobedience. Imagine a basketball game where the referees never blew the whistle or called a penalty. How long would it take the players to figure out that the rules no longer applied? The game would degenerate into a brawl. The fans might like it, but do we want our children to act that way?

Children raised in permissive homes usually have a terrible time accepting responsibility in their lives. To them, responsibility is always someone else's responsibility. It is too bad that so many of our youth have to *leave* home to learn what they should have learned *at* home—that they *are* responsible for the consequences of their decisions. When they are exposed to law later in life, they rarely submit to it, rebelling against it instead. Depending on how long they have been on the "love without law" program, the "love" may be as eroded as the "law." Disobedience has never been conducive to loving relationships, any more than wickedness ever was happiness (Alma 41:10). So parents who eliminate law or penalty for the sake of love, ultimately defeat their own purpose and usually end up with neither. Practicing love without law is a temptation for all parents who love their children, because love is the fun part about having kids whereas enforcing the law is no fun at all. What we need to remember is that no one is more loving or compassionate than God, and yet He still punishes His children.

Another reason some parents give for not punishing their children is that they are fearful of committing abuse. Abuse must be avoided like the plague, because it can destroy almost any relationship. But only *extreme* punishment is abusive and every parent has the obligation to administer justice without going to an abusive extreme. But a permissive extreme should not be adopted out of fear of committing abuse. Is it right to embrace one extreme for fear of committing another? Do we quit feeding our children out of fear that we might accidentally give them something unhealthy? An opposite extreme does not usually solve a problem. It creates another instead. The most common problem with punishment is not *abuse;* it is *disuse.* It is a parent's duty *not* to waive penalty, because the Father who serves as our parental role model does not waive it.

> For I the Lord cannot look upon sin with the least degree of allowance. [D&C 1:31]
>
> Therefore I command you to repent—repent, lest I smite you by the rod of my mouth, and by my wrath, and by

Chapter 11   Satan's War on the Family

my anger, and your sufferings be sore—how sore you know not, how exquisite you know not, yea, how hard to bear you know not. [D&C 19:15]

Who am I that made man, saith the Lord, that will hold him guiltless that obeys not my commandments? [D&C 58:30]

How to Raise an Irresponsible Child

To raise an irresponsible child you simply try to do what Satan did: you destroy his agency. You cannot actually destroy his agency, since agency is God given, but you can destroy his *understanding* of it. You can completely distort his perception of agency and how it works by making him think he is not accountable for his behavior.

Raising an irresponsible child is not as easy as it may seem. It usually takes a lot of work. The basic principle is simple enough—just let him do as he pleases and make sure he does not have to face any negative consequences for his negative behaviors.

It is best to start when he is an infant. It will be your job to see that his every *want* is satisfied, not just his *needs*. No matter how tired he is, do not let him cry himself to sleep. You must rock him to sleep. Whenever he wants something, get it for him, even if he is capable of getting it for himself. If he is misbehaving or disobeying, you may *tell* him what is right and wrong, but you must never *enforce* it. Use any manipulative mind games at your disposal, especially distraction, but never punishment.

You must be willing to do things for him that he is not willing to do for himself. Carry him even when he can walk by himself. Spoon-feed him long after he is capable of using a spoon by himself. Dress him even after he is old enough to dress himself. Make sure, however, that *he* gets the credit for the things you do for him. Be sure to do his homework for him if he won't do it himself. Cover for him by lying to teachers about why he was absent from school.

You must be patient. Raising an irresponsible child requires a firm belief that he will eventually grow out of his rebelliousness. He probably won't, but it helps you to believe that he will. If you ever start to feel guilty about the way he is acting, excuses are an excellent remedy. Learn to blame others for his problems. Friends, teachers, and Church leaders are all very handy targets. You might also blame some medical condition or genetic disorder, but you will need to be familiar with the popular psychological vernacular of the day. This will require extra work for you, but it can be very comforting.

Never say "no" to him and mean it. He will begin to understand that your saying "no" the first time means for him to try again. Saying "no" a second time encourages him to persist in his stubbornness, while saying it a third time means that you have almost given up. It is best to give in after the third "no" or else he might start to believe that you mean what you say. This would be a serious mistake. He could learn to be responsible if he knows that you mean what you say. This develops trust and must be avoided at all costs.

Don't worry, trust is easy to avoid. All you have to do is make sure that your actions do *not* match your words. Doing so is an attribute of godhood (Moses 4:30) and the fundamental principle upon which we can develop faith in God. To emulate this would be to establish a vital relationship of trust with your child. Trust is your greatest enemy. Most irresponsible children distrust their parents. You must make sure you do not keep your promises, especially any promises about punishments. To make sure you never make good on a threat, it helps to exaggerate the threat to a degree you are not willing to carry out.

To do these things effectively and consistently requires that you

Chapter 11 ~ Satan's War on the Family

adopt and maintain certain beliefs. If you do not sustain your faith in these false principles, you will be less likely to maintain the diligence required to raise an irresponsible child. You must believe that the consequences of letting him fail will be too harsh for him to endure. You must believe that he will someday learn to make good decisions if you consistently reward him for making bad decisions. Let your love for him justify your permissiveness in protecting him from the consequences of his bad choices. Convince yourself that he will someday love and respect you for all the nice things you've done for him. You must believe that children who are punished cannot feel loved and that the trauma of any punishment will permanently damage your relationship with them. It helps to believe that entertainment is the key to their happiness. You must believe that when they cannot entertain themselves, then it is your responsibility to provide more entertainment for them. You must believe that professors who write textbooks know more about parenting than prophets who wrote scriptures. Your most fundamental belief will be that punishment means force and force is Satan's plan.

This method will work most of the time. The problem is that occasionally your child will learn to be responsible regardless of your best efforts to teach him otherwise. He could learn responsible behavior from reading the scriptures and gaining a testimony of the gospel of Jesus Christ. He might also learn it in church or seminary, but not usually. Only occasionally can outside influences compensate for failure in the home. If anything is going to teach him to be responsible, it is usually the hard consequences of life. Most prodigal sons were not taught accountability and only return when they've hit bottom.

How to Raise a Responsible Child

To raise a responsible child you simply try to do what Heavenly Father did: you preserve his agency. You can actually only help him to *understand* his agency, since it is God given, and always in effect. You can increase his understanding of agency and how it works by teaching him to accept the fact that *he* is accountable for his behavior.

Raising a responsible child is not as easy as it may seem. It usually takes a lot of work. The basic principle is simple enough—just make sure that he appropriately experiences different consequences for different behaviors.

It is best to start when he is an infant. Whenever he wants something it will be your job to see that his every *need* is satisfied but not always his *wants*. When you know he is fed, changed, and healthy, yet very tired, do not think you always have to rock him to sleep. He will learn that he can go to sleep without crying. If he wants something, get it for him *only* if he asks nicely or cannot get it for himself. Expect him to get something for *you* occasionally. If he is misbehaving or disobeying, first tell him the rules, then explain the consequences of each decision. Let him choose, and then make sure he experiences the promised consequence. Avoid using distraction. Use appropriate punishment when necessary. This is not manipulation.

You must *not* make a habit of doing things for him that he is capable of doing for himself. Do not make a habit of carrying him when he can walk by himself. Do not spoon-feed him after he is capable of using a spoon by himself. Expect him to dress himself when he is capable. Make sure, however, that *he* gets the credit for the

Chapter 11 — Satan's War on the Family

things he does for himself. Help him with his homework if he needs it, but do not do it for him. If he won't do it for him himself, let him get the grade he deserves. Never cover for him by lying to teachers about why he was absent from school.

You must be patient. Raising a responsible child requires a firm belief that your training will avoid serious rebellion. It will not always avoid rebellion, but more often than not it will. You must not feel guilty about the way he is acting, regardless of his excuses. Do not let him blame others for his problems. Teach him that neither friends, teachers, or Church leaders can make his decisions for him or take his consequences. If he has some medical condition or genetic disorder, expect him to do his best in spite of his disadvantage. This may require extra work for him, but his weakness can actually become his strength (Ether 12:27).

When you say "no" to him, mean what you say. He will begin to understand that your saying "no" the first time means that he should trust you enough to not do it again. Saying "no" the second time comes with your last warning of certain consequences that will result if the behavior is repeated. Do not say "no" a third time. If he does it again, deliver the promised consequences. Do this consistently, and he will know that you mean what you say. To do otherwise would be a serious mistake. He could learn to be irresponsible if he knows that you do not mean what you say. This develops distrust and must be avoided at all costs.

Don't worry, trust takes time to develop. But all you really have to do is make sure that your actions match your words. Doing so is an attribute of godhood (Moses 4:30) and the fundamental principle upon which we can develop faith in God. To emulate this will establish a vital relationship of trust with your child. Trust is your greatest asset. Most responsible children trust their parents. Just make sure you keep your promises concerning both rewards and punishments. Always make good on a threat. Never make empty threats or exaggerate the threat to a degree that you're not willing to carry it out.

To do these things effectively and consistently requires that you adopt and maintain certain beliefs. If you do not sustain your faith in the principles of accountability, you will be less likely to maintain the diligence required to raise a responsible child. You must believe that the consequences of letting him fail can be the very experiences he needs to learn to make better decisions. You must believe that he will eventually learn to make good decisions if you consistently refuse to reward him for making bad decisions. Let your love for him justify *not* protecting him from the consequences of his bad choices. Have the conviction that he will return your love and respect for your teaching him things that give him all the advantages he enjoys. You must believe that children who are appropriately punished will not forget they are loved, and that no trauma from appropriate punishment will permanently damage your relationship with them. You must believe that their doing what is right is the key to their happiness. You must believe that they *can* entertain themselves, even without technology, and that opportunities to do so can teach them to be creative and productive. You must believe that prophets who wrote scriptures know more about parenting than professors who write textbooks. Your most fundamental belief will be that agency includes experiencing different results for different choices. It will help to remember that avoiding accountability was Satan's plan.

This method will work most of the time. The problem is that occasionally your child will become irresponsible regardless of your best efforts to teach him otherwise. He could learn irresponsible behavior in spite of reading the scriptures and even in spite of having a testimony of the gospel of Jesus Christ. He might also learn to be irresponsible in church or seminary, but not usually. Only occasion-

Chapter 11 ~ SATAN'S WAR ON THE FAMILY

ally will outside influences overpower well-taught accountability in the home. If he does become rebellious and irresponsible, it is usually because of his own hardened heart. But remember that a prodigal son who was taught accountability doesn't usually have to hit bottom before he returns.

Chapter 12

"War" Stories

Satan's war on agency is an effort to eliminate penalty. If we are to become like God, then we must learn to use punishment appropriately. The War in Heaven has now shifted to the home front, but the war is not against our children, it is against Satan and his doctrine. It is against all the modern philosophies teaching us that penalty is always destructive to relationships.

In a psychology class, I once spoke up for the appropriate use of penalty, saying that it need not destroy relationships if administered properly. My professor, with a little smirk on his face, asked me what he thought was an unanswerable question. "OK then tell me," he said, "how much can you punish a child before you've destroyed the relationship?" The question was intended as a trap for people like me who dare to believe in the "archaic" principle of penalty.

His question is like asking this: "How much can you withdraw from your bank account before you are overdrawn?" How much you can withdraw depends entirely on how much you have deposited. If you have made plenty of deposits, you can afford to make withdrawals when you need to. By analogy, if you have made regular deposits of affection, your children will not forget that they are loved, even when they receive some correction and are made to accept the unpleasant consequences of wrong decisions. With enough loving affection in the bank, penalty can actually be very effective, because when they know they are loved, the risk to the relationship will be *theirs*, not yours. Thus withdrawals can actually be investments, paying dividends for years to come.

Principles are best understood through experience. This final chapter will relate a few stories I have experienced that are particularly memorable with regards to the positive effects of preserving agency by holding children accountable through the use of punishment.

The Murphy's

Early in my marriage and in a new ward, I wanted to know how a certain family, I'll call them the Murphy's, could raise such a fine bunch of kids as they had. There were twelve children in that family. They lived in a three-bedroom home with wall to wall bunk beds. The children were personable, friendly, respectful, fun loving, happy, smart, and responsible. They each had their unique challenges, but there was not a rebel among them. I honestly never spoke to one of the Murphy children without being impressed at their maturity. I had three of them in my seminary classes, so I got to know them quite well.

They took up a whole center bench at church every Sunday, and sat on the second row, right up front. Possibly the most amazing thing to me was the behavior of the children at church. They lined up on their bench with mom and dad sitting together, not on either end or at some strategic location in the middle. They didn't need a different arrangement because the kids were all reverent. If the younger ones

Chapter 12 ~ "War" Stories

got noisy, the older ones would correct them or separate them. The parents rarely ever even looked over to see what was going on. They knew the older ones would deal with any problems. Once in a while one of the little ones would start fussing or crying like little ones do. One of the older children would take the child out. It was no big deal. Only if it was serious would mom or dad get involved.

Brother and Sister Murphy were my heros and I tried to tell them so. I so admired their family that if I had not seen and known them myself, it would have been hard to believe they were real. I wanted my kids to be like theirs. I studied their family to try to find the secret of their success. By observation and elimination I discovered that the secret was not the number of children, the second row bench at church or their very humble circumstances in life, but I just couldn't figure out what it was.

One day I decided to ask Mr. Murphy how he turned out such good kids with not a single rebel. He humbly assured me that they were far from perfect. I told him I understood, but that I also knew they were a very unusual bunch and had something very special, and I wanted to know how he did it. What were the principles upon which he based his very successful efforts to raise responsible children? His first answer was a tremendous disappointment to me: "Well I don't really know. My wife and I just try to do what's right and teach them what's right. I can't really identify anything special for you."

I already knew they usually had family prayers and family nights, but they were not overly organized. Sister Murphy even told us about one morning at breakfast when she noticed that one of the children was missing and nobody at the table knew where she was. It wasn't until the second or third shift at the breakfast table, that someone remembered that she had spent the night at a friends house. Obviously, organization alone was not their secret.

I realized that I had to get specific in order to get an answer, so I asked Mr. Murphy this question: "Tell me then, what do you do to keep your kids quiet during church?" He almost failed me again, saying, "Well I don't know, they just learn to be quiet. I can tell you what I don't do." "What?" I quickly asked. He said, "I don't take them out in the lobby and let them run free." He had my attention because that is exactly what I had been doing along with every other young couple. "What do you do then?" I continued. "I take them out and sit them on my lap and hold them until they are quiet. Then we go back in and I set them down and expect them to behave. Letting them run around is exactly what they want. They learn to misbehave if they know you're going to give them what they want every time they do. And if I have to take them out a second time, I give them a swat on their backside. They figure out pretty fast that sitting quietly in church isn't so bad."

At that moment a light went on for me. One principle was finally clear. *It is wrong to reward negative behavior.* Satan wanted to do it, but God wouldn't do it and we shouldn't do it either. Parents who make a habit of it often reap the sad results of practicing a false philosophy. The Murphy's did nothing but practice the principles of accountability. It was such a habit of their lives that they couldn't even identify the principles. They only knew what to do because they had been raised that way. It wasn't complicated—they simply held their children accountable for their choices, and as a result, their children learned to make pretty good choices.

Through the years I have observed hundreds of examples and nonexamples of parents practicing the principles of accountability. It is not a perfect correlation, but by far, most of the responsible kids come from homes where they are held responsible. On the other

Chapter 12 ~ "War" Stories

hand, the rebellious and disrespectful kids have been *allowed*, if not actually *trained*, to be rebellious.

The Old Couch

As my children grew they had their moments when they needed correction. It was never pleasant for them, but it was never intended to be. By definition, punishment must be "opposite to the plan of happiness" (Alma 42:16). Punishment usually took the form of verbal correction or privilege denial, which sometimes resulted in tears. I usually held and comforted them in their tears, but I did not withdraw the promised penalty.

At times the crying would go on longer than called for by the penalty. When the tears were no longer sorrow "unto repentance" (Mormon 2:13), but an attempt to punish me, I sent them to their room to finish crying so they didn't make the rest of the family unhappy. I would say, "When you decide to stop crying and be happy again, you can come back out and join the family." Sometimes it took a while, but they always stopped sooner or later. When they did, it was their decision, putting the responsibility for their own happiness squarely upon them.

The greatest challenges in their younger years were the inter sibling battles. One would make fun of, mistreat, manipulate, or torment one of the others. For years either my wife or myself would be both judge and jury when they presented their cases to us. We tried to hear the arguments fairly and then make a decision on the basis of what we thought was right. But the decision too often went in favor of the older siblings, who had the advantage of being better able to articulate their case, or who were often better actors. Besides assuming too much responsibility for their choices, we were making little lawyers out of them.

Not liking the direction of this, I decided upon a change in plan. The next time two of them came to me with a mutual grievance, I told them that it wasn't *my* problem. It was *their* problem, and they needed to learn how to solve their own problems. I told them both to go sit on the couch until they had *both* agreed on a solution to *their* problem.

This changed everything! That old couch is where my children learned to communicate, to solve problems in a fair and reasonable manner and even to love each other. Why did it work? Because I put the responsibility for their happiness where it belonged—upon them, not me. This is not to say that it was easy. Sometimes there was "weeping, wailing and gnashing of teeth" (Alma 40:13) for hours on that old couch. No longer could the older one just outsmart the younger, because the younger wouldn't agree to anything that was not acceptable. Occasionally I would intervene to give some direction and advice, but mostly I left them alone because the unpleasantness of the time on the couch, was punishment enough, and self inflicted. It worked, and in time they learned to resolve issues quickly and fairly, without the need for any couch time.

One payday came not long ago when my youngest, then 14, had been asked by a friend to babysit her two-year-old. She brought her boy over to our house, but as soon as she began to leave, he began to cry. It got louder as she closed the door and was a full tantrum by the time my daughter took him by the hand and walked him across the room. I was in the adjacent room and available if she needed me, but I did not volunteer to help. The child was *her* responsibility, not mine. Besides, I wanted to see how she would handle the situation.

After about 10 minutes I suddenly noticed that the house was quiet. I looked behind me and saw my daughter doing her homework at the kitchen table, but the boy was not with her. I didn't say a word,

Chapter 12 ~ "War" Stories

but I got up and went to look for him. I figured that if he was quiet, it was because he found something interesting to destroy, and if so, my daughter was going to be held responsible for not watching him more closely. I went into the front room and there he was, sound asleep on the couch. I went back into the kitchen and asked my daughter how she got him to go to sleep. She replied, "I just told him he had to stay on the couch until he quit crying, and then he could come in and join the family." That was definitely daddy's payday.

Are You Happy?

The plan of salvation is called the "plan of happiness" in the Book of Mormon (Alma 42:8, 16). It also says that "wickedness never was happiness" (Alma 41:10). These simple principles were very helpful in teaching my children right from wrong. Using these as standards I learned that instead of just telling them what was right and wrong, I should also tell them why.

Countless times through the years I told them the reason something is right is that it makes us happy, and the reason something is wrong is that it makes us unhappy. I do not know why this is so hard for us to learn, but it is. The natural man in each of us wants to believe that our unhappiness is someone else's fault. But mature thinking begins when we accept the fact that we are responsible for our own happiness. Only then do we really learn to use our agency to our advantage, making choices that will make us happy, and avoiding choices that will make us unhappy. I taught this to my children as they grew.

I would often use times when my children were being selfish and causing each other misery as teaching moments. I would have two of them standing before me with their eyebrows down and their lower lips stuck out as far as they could go, often already in tears, complaining to me about how mean the other had been. I did my best to judge who was right and wrong, but I tried to expand their vision with a few questions. "Are you happy?" I would ask. They would shake their little heads admitting they were not. "Then what does that tell you about what you have done?" They didn't really understand this the first hundred times we had this conversation, but I was persistent, having faith and hope that some day they would get it. In time they did, and since then they have usually been pretty honest about admitting that their selfishness and mistreatment of a brother or sister had not made them happy.

I didn't always wait for a problem to arise to take an opportunity to teach this concept. Occasionally while they were sitting on the floor happily playing with each other, I would stop and ask them if they were happy. When they assured me they were, I would ask them why? At first this puzzled them, and their reply was that they weren't doing anything wrong. I agreed but asked them what they *were* doing. At first they could only think of wrong things they were *not* doing, but in time I helped them understand that they were happy because they were doing something good. They were treating each other well, sharing their toys and cooperating. *This*, I told them, was why they were happy. So when they *were not* happy, reminding them of when they *were*, made the reasons much more clear.

Then came the day that my oldest got wise to her father's happiness philosophy. After tormenting and hitting her little brother, I asked her if it made her happy to make her brother unhappy. Thinking to thwart my philosophy, she replied that it did. She said it was fun making him cry. I knew then that it was time to teach the next principle. I explained to her the difference between immediate and ultimate consequences. I explained that in time such treatment would damage her relationship with him. I also explained that it was my responsibility to teach her right from wrong, and that if the ultimate natural consequences were not enough to teach her, then I would need to impose some immediate consequences that would. I said that if I did not teach her right from wrong, she would grow up learning to do wrong and it would result in an unhappy life. So the consequence I had to impose was to give her a spanking, which I had always promised my children if they resorted to violence with one another.

She started to cry before the spanking began, so I didn't have to swat her very hard. I held her for a while afterwards to comfort her and reassure her of my love. After a while I told her she should go finish crying in her room and she was welcome to come out when she was done. After a short while the crying stopped, but she didn't come out immediately. When she did come out, she walked over to me, put her arms around me, and said, "Thank you for spanking me daddy."

A Chat with Mr. Freedom

In my nineteen years as a seminary teacher I have had a lot of conversations with the parents of my students. Some understood the principles of agency and others did not. The following are two typical phone conversations I have had with parents, Mr. Freedom and Mr. Law, named after the philosophies they respectively embraced.

Brother Wright: Hello, Mr. Freedom? This is Brother Wright. I'm Darren's seminary teacher.

Mr. Freedom: Yes, Darren has told us about you, and frankly I'm surprised that you would even call.

Brother Wright: I don't know what you've heard, but I'm willing to discuss any concerns you may have.

Mr. Freedom: Well from what I hear it probably wouldn't do any good anyway, but what's on your mind?

Brother Wright: I'm calling because Darren has been missing seminary lately. I've spoken with him about it and haven't been able to influence him to attend regularly. I was hoping you could help.

Mr. Freedom: Well he just doesn't want to be in your class. He doesn't like you, the way you teach, or the way you treat him. Besides, I can't force him to be there anyway. A lot of those kids are forced to be there and it only makes them rebel. We shouldn't be forcing our religion on our children, because that was Satan's plan. We should let them choose for themselves. Wasn't that Jesus' plan?

Brother Wright: I'm sorry Darren has some negative feelings about me. I honestly don't know how I might have offended him. Forcing him to attend seminary is not an option for anyone, but Darren made a commitment to be in seminary, and I am only trying to influence him to keep his commitment.

Mr. Freedom: Influence? You threatened to give him an "Incomplete" if he didn't come to class. I'd call that forcing him. You can't make him want to be there by threatening him. He has to make that decision for himself, without any threats from you or anyone else.

Brother Wright: I have no choice but to withhold credit if he doesn't attend. That is a policy of the Church Educational System. The Church also has a liability concern about students who continually miss class. If he doesn't attend, I am also obligated to drop him from the roll and inform the school that his released time class has been revoked.

Mr. Freedom: Well, Brother Wright, it's attitudes like yours that are the reason why my son is having problems in the Church. You should just be glad that Darren ever comes into your class at all. It's hypocrites like you that chase people away from the Church. Jesus didn't exclude anyone from His church. If you loved your students

Chapter 12 ~ "War" Stories

you wouldn't treat them that way. You're supposed to care about those kids not kick them out!

In cases like this, it is sometimes hard to know who is more irresponsible, the parent or the child. Mr. Freedom was a big part of the reason why Darren was having problems understanding responsibility. The sad thing is that kids like Darren usually have to leave home before they figure it out. Consequences will teach them what their parents do not. Contrast this with another conversation.

A Chat with Mr. Law

Brother Wright: Hello, Mr. Law? This is Brother Wright. I'm John's seminary teacher.

Mr. Law: Yes, John has told us about you. What can I do for you?

Brother Wright: I'm calling because John has been skipping seminary lately. I've spoken with him about it and haven't been able to influence him to attend regularly. I was hoping you could help.

Mr. Law: Well, I'm glad you called Brother Wright. I didn't know John was skipping seminary. Of course we can't force him to attend, but I think I can assure you that he *will* be there from now on.

Brother Wright: That's great, but how can you be sure that he won't miss class again?

Mr. Law: Well, you know that car that he drives?

Brother Wright: His Mustang?

Mr. Law: No *my* Mustang.

Brother Wright: Oh, I thought it was his.

Mr. Law: So did he. But tonight I'll remind him that it belongs to me because I am going to take the keys for a week.

Brother Wright: I see. How will he get to school?

Mr. Law: That's his problem, but he has several options. He can get a ride with a friend, take the bus, ride his bike, or walk. It's up to him. Driving the Mustang was a privilege conditioned upon his attendance at seminary. He knew the consequences. He made his choice and now he will lose that privilege for a while. I think a week without the Mustang will get the message across. If not, we can try two weeks or a month. John is a smart boy and a pretty good kid, so I think he'll make the right decision.

Brother Wright: John is a good kid. He was certainly born of goodly parents. What can I do to help?

Mr. Law: Well, you just keep trying to be a goodly teacher and I'll keep trying to be a goodly dad. The rest is up to John.

The Lost Sheep, Coin and Son

A desperate mother called me about a seminary situation with one of her sons. In the course of our conversation, the discussion turned to her oldest son who was about 18 and out of high school. He was a very rebellious young man, who drank and used drugs along with who knows what else. The mother's grief was indescribable. She had no idea what to do for him. She and her husband had loved him, taught him and been active in the Church, and yet they were losing him to sin and rebellion. He refused to go to church with them, continued to cause contention in the home, and maybe worst of all, he was trying to destroy the faith of his younger brothers by influencing them to live as he did.

She and her husband considered telling him to leave but were afraid that they would make matters worse and didn't know if it was right. He threatened them that if they kicked him out, he would do even worse things and never return. So they succumbed to his

Chapter 12 ~ "War" Stories

terrorism and tolerated his destruction of the spiritual environment they had spent a lifetime building.

In an effort to help her make a decision, we discussed the War in Heaven, Satan's plan being one of freedom rather than force, and how it applies today. I also suggested that we read Luke 15 together, agreeing that she should do whatever the Savior would do. In that chapter Jesus told three parables about three things that get lost. The first tells of the lost sheep, representing people who wander away from the truth for no particular reason. In the parable the shepherd has the responsibility to go out after the sheep and bring it home if at all possible. He does so and rejoices with his friends over the lost sheep that was found (Luke 15:3–7).

The next parable tells about a lost coin, representing someone who is lost because of the carelessness of another. The responsibility of finding this coin is upon the woman to who carelessly lost it. She does so and rejoices with her friends when it is found (Luke 15:8–10).

The last parable is about a lost son, known as the prodigal son. This young man did not just innocently wander off, nor was he offended by the carelessness of another. He was a rebel. He demanded his portion of his father's inheritance, left home and "wasted his substance with riotous living" (Luke 15:13). Unlike in the other situations, no responsibility to attempt to bring him back was placed on anyone. Everyone simply let him go, not knowing if they would ever see him again, much less, if he would ever repent.

I told this grieving mother that a time does come to let a prodigal son go. The time even comes when rebels must be cast out, just like Lucifer was. It may be that part of the reason Father cast him out was to preserve as many of His other children as He could. Lucifer was not content to rebel alone, he wanted to influence others to do the same. "This is where I would draw the line," I told her. "I wouldn't allow any of my children to intentionally destroy the faith of the others if I could prevent it." I assured her that only she and her husband could make that decision. I encouraged her to prayerfully decide if and when that time should come, but that they were justified if it should come to that.

The young man in the parable did return, but only after he had spent his money and was so hungry that the food he fed the pigs looked good to him. Only then did he finally hit bottom, come to his senses and decide to return and beg for forgiveness. The most touching part of the parable is when the father saw his son "a great way off," ran to him, embraced him and welcomed him home (Luke 15:20). The prodigal son came home because he never doubted that he was *loved*. His problem was that he didn't like the *laws*. I told this mother that there was no guarantee that her son would come back, but that he was not likely to "hit bottom" as long as he could do as he pleased in her home, all the while enjoying free room and board.

Most of us bounce back when we hit bottom. We differ in that each person must individually decide where the bottom is. The more humble ones have a low tolerance for misery and repent very quickly. The more prideful ones are determined to show everybody how much pain they can endure. Some of these sink very low before they will admit that *they* have made *themselves* unhappy and decide to change. I told the mother that as long as her son was living at home, he was being protected from the very consequences that might bring him back. Obviously they didn't want to lose him, but in a way, they had already lost him and might actually be prolonging the time of his return.

About a year later this woman called me again to tell me what had happened. She and her husband had decided to tell their son to leave and that he would be welcome to come back only upon the condition that he abide by the family rules. This would include a change not only in his behavior but in his attitude. She said it was the hardest thing they had ever done and the whole family wept over his departure. Months went by and this prodigal son also came home. On his own he had finally figured out that *his* kind of freedom was not all that he hoped it would be. He found himself with no job, no money, no friends, no self-respect and no happiness. He agreed to keep the family rules. A change occurred as he opened his heart and his scriptures. To make a long and painful story short, through her tears she thanked me and told me he was preparing for a mission.

The Solder Gun

My wife and I became friends with a couple who had several young children. The youngest, whom we will call Eric, had quite a behavior problem. As I recall, he was about four years old. Whenever they came to our home for a visit, Eric would run around being destructive, completely ignoring commands, warnings and threats from his parents. He was well loved, so love was not the problem. His parents also gave him the law, but he refused to comply, running instead from place to place causing problems for everyone he met. The only time he was quiet was when he was plotting his next disaster.

The problem was that Eric didn't trust his parents because they constantly lied to him. They told him they would punish him if he disobeyed "one more time," but they never did. Since they never did what they promised, Eric came to know that they didn't mean what they said. After countless broken promises day after day, what other conclusion could he come to? As a result, Eric didn't trust them, and since there were no negative consequences to his behavior, he did as he pleased. Since he lived in the University of Freedom, he did what *he* enjoyed without regard for anyone elses feelings.

On one occasion I thought I would try the old distraction technique in an effort to get him to settle down. I was working at my desk on an electronics project, soldering a circuit board. Eric was fascinated as he watched the solder gun heat up, melt the solder and send a puff of smoke into the air. It seemed to be working because he was actually quiet for a while. As his curiosity got the best of him, he decided to touch the solder gun to see what it felt like. As his finger came toward the hot tip of the gun, I pulled it away and said, "Oh Eric, don't touch that. It will burn you." He drew back his little hand, but about a minute later he reached up to touch it again. Again I pulled away the solder gun and said, with a little more seriousness in my voice, "Eric, don't touch it. It is very hot and it *will* burn you." Eric pulled back again, but after a few minutes he again reached up to touch the solder gun. For the third time I pulled it back and spoke to him very sternly, "Eric, if you touch this it will burn you *very* badly and you will cry *very* hard."

If he had been my own child I would have let him get burned that third time he tried to touch it. The problem was that his dad was sitting on the couch watching the whole thing, and I didn't want to jeopardize our friendship. While pondering over whether losing that friendship was a deterrent or an incentive, Eric's little finger came up again to touch the tip of the solder gun. I knew why he was doing it. It was because he was curious and he didn't trust me. He didn't trust anyone who warned him of negative consequences. There was only one way to win his trust on this occasion. So as his little finger came up, I let him touch it. It took just about a second for the little puff of smoke to rise up from the end of his finger. He screamed and cried for a good while as his dad held him and called him an idiot.

Our friendship survived and a week or so later we were having dinner at their house. As usual, Eric was running all over the place, jumping on all the furniture, throwing things and yelling. This went on for 15 or 20 minutes while his dad was continually telling him to "stop it" and to "settle down." Finally, I called to him in a firm voice saying, "Eric!" He stopped and looked at me. I tightened my lips, gave him a stern look and simply shook my head. He got down off the couch and sat quietly for a few minutes, then got one of his favorite books, crawled up on my lap, and I read it to him. His father sat in amazement and finally said to me. "Wow, that was amazing. What's your secret?" I replied, "Have you got a solder gun?"

A Cheek for a Cheek

A new ward brought new friends. We got to know a large family, we will call the Landons. They were good, faithful people, the kind that always stay to clean up after activities. They often invited us over to their house for ice cream or something freshly baked.

Their children had some interesting habits. Let's just say that their problem solving skills had not yet developed. Conflicts and fights broke out frequently. There was a lot of contention, yelling, hitting and crying. The older ones usually got their way only because they did most of the hitting while the younger ones did most of the crying. To me it was chaotic; to them it was all very normal. The parents were not uninvolved. They yelled at the kids to stop teasing, hitting, being selfish or whatever, but they did not intervene until something was serious.

The fateful event occurred at a ward dinner only a few months after we arrived. I had gotten to know most of the Landon children, having a particular fondness for the younger ones who were fun to hold, hug, tickle and play with. One boy about six years old, we'll call him Gary, was quite full of energy that night. I was sitting at one of the round tables, talking to other friends and waiting for dinner, which was being served. Gary was running around and around the table pretending to be some super hero. It was not a problem until he almost tripped someone with a plate full of food. Instead of saying excuse me or apologizing, he just bounced off and kept going.

His parents were in the kitchen helping out, so they weren't there to deal with the situation. Gary and I were friends and his parents had left him in my care before, so I decided it wouldn't be inappropriate for me to expect from him what they would expect. I told him it was time to settle down and take a seat so he would not get in another person's way. He ignored me and kept going, running even faster and making even more noise than before. Again I told him that he needed to stop running around, sit up and get ready to eat. Again he ignored me and kept going. I was done telling him, so on his next trip around I held out my arm at waist level and he ran right into it. I then scooped him up into my lap and said, "Gary, you need to sit still now because you are causing trouble for the people serving the dinner." He said not a word as he tried to twist away, get down off my lap and continue running around. But I held him tighter and would not let him go, again telling him that I would not let him go until he calmed down. He looked me straight in the eye with a casual coldness, cocked back his right arm and slapped me hard across the left cheek. To Gary this was perfectly normal behavior. It was how I had seen him deal with situations at home many times.

There was much for me to consider at this point, not the least of which was my relationship with his parents. But my primary concern was for Gary. I had grown very fond of him so I did not want to lose my relationship with him. I thought he liked me as well, but he needed to learn that slapping people is not a good way to preserve meaningful relationships. He was under the impression that resorting to physical violence was an appropriate method for obtaining what he wanted in life or avoiding something he didn't want to do. My greatest concern was for Gary's future. It was more important than our present relationship, and should he continue in his behavior, very serious consequences would await him as he grew older. Gary also needed to learn respect for adults who only had his interests at heart. But how to teach him this was the question. All of these thoughts went through my mind in no more than two seconds.

Within two seconds I concluded that there was no better time than the present. I chose to take a teaching moment, for Gary's sake, even if it cost me my friendship with him and his parents. I remained calm, looked him in the eye, and slapped him across the left cheek just a little harder than he had slapped me. I remained calm as I waited for his response, not knowing if he would slap me again or not, but I left him a clear shot just in case that was his desire. It wasn't.

His expression was one of shock and total surprise. I suppose no one had ever delivered such a consequence to him before—no adult anyway, or he probably would not have slapped me in the first place. In about five seconds his surprise gave way to tears, and when he struggled to get down and run to his parents, I let him go. I think the sting to his pride was more painful than that on his cheek, at least I hoped so. Be that as it may, he remained quiet the rest of the evening.

My main concern now was my relationship with Gary. I didn't know what he would do the next time he saw me. Would he run from me, avoid me or treat me with rudeness? I couldn't know because it was up to him, not me. He knew I loved him, I just didn't know if he regretted what he had done to me and would want to resume our friendship. It was all up to him, so I concluded to treat him as if nothing had happened and let *him* decide the level of our relationship.

The inevitable moment came that Sunday. I walked around one corner in the church hallway just as he came around another, heading toward me. I will never forget the feelings in my heart for that little boy as he did not run away, but rather, he ran all the way down the hall, jumped into my arms and gave me the biggest hug he ever had. We have never had another problem, and his parents are still my friends.

Tonya in the Nursery

We moved into a ward full of young families. I'm not sure, but it seemed like half the ward was in primary. I *am* sure that the ward had four nurseries because my wife and I were called to begin the fourth one. When they opened up our nursery, the other three quickly donated their top four problem kids to us. We had twelve little rowdy toddlers, including a number of pretty serious criers.

At first I was sure that I was being punished for something I had done wrong and had forgotten to confess. But within a few weeks I grew to love them all. My wife would teach them and feed them cookies while I would hold the criers, give them stickers and clip their fingernails. I would set the criers on my lap, and tell them that everything was going to be fine, and that as soon as the crying stopped the playing could resume. It often took ten to fifteen minutes after their moms dropped them off for them to settle down. Meanwhile I told the moms and dads not to come back for two hours. If anything serious happened, I would bring their child to them. The kids would cry until they figured out that I wasn't lying, that everything *was* fine, and that they were only making themselves unhappy by continuing to cry. As soon as they quit, I let them go play with their friends, but not before. Some criers even became screamers, but I still wouldn't let them go until they stopped because I refused to reward negative behavior. Week after week went by and there was less and less crying because they could see that resistance was futile and that happiness was the reward for self-control.

Chapter 12 ～ "War" Stories

Then came Tonya, and that *was* her real name. Her parents were coming back into activity in the Church and she was their main problem. She was a momma's girl, and a serious screamer. They put her in nursery #1, then #2, #3, and finally ours. Each nursery resulted in failure because Tonya screamed until the leaders gave up and took her back to her mother, which was exactly what she wanted. After three nursery experiences, Tonya had learned the system well and knew how to beat it.

We were privately told that her parents had decided that if Tonya could not stay in our nursery, they would quit going to church again, and just keep her at home. It was causing too much stress on the parents to continue trying to go to church with Tonya so upset all the time. When Tonya came in, she was fine as long as her mother was with her. This gave me time to tell her mother the strategy—not to come back for two hours. She warned me what would happen, but I assured her that I would be fine.

Her warning turned out to be real. When her mother left the screams began, so I held her like all the others. Tonya not only screamed but she hit me and kicked me on the shins with those cowboy boots of hers. I didn't spank her (as I would have my own child). I held her tightly and confined her arms and legs whenever she used them to attack me. But the confinement made her even more angry and she screamed louder and struggled harder, but it was the only other consequence I could think of. I kept a calm tone of voice and told her that I wouldn't hold down her arms and legs if she would stop trying to hit and kick me. She quit kicking long enough to regain her freedom, only to brake her promise and resume the kicking. This happened several times, but she finally gave up the violence because the confinement wasn't worth it.

After about an hour and a half she cried herself into exhaustion and finally took a little nap in my lap. When she woke up I asked her if she wanted to get down and play with the other kids, several of whom were former criers and had come over to comfort her. She started crying and fighting again, but this time she gave it up after about ten minutes. When she quit I let her down. She tried to go out the door but I told her she had to wait for her mom to come before she could leave. She started to cry again. I asked her if she wanted to sit on my lap again. She stopped crying. She sulked in the corner for a while and finally found something to play with just about the time her mom came in. I can't describe the joy on her mother's face to see her little girl playing with the other children instead of throwing a tantrum.

The next week it started all over. The difference was that the crying only lasted about forty-five minutes. The next week she only cried for about twenty minutes, and the next week maybe five. Each time, though, she only gained her freedom when she stopped crying. When the next week came, her mother brought her to the door. Tonya ran into the room and into my arms and gave me a big hug, then went to play with the other kids. After that, the only time she ever spent in my lap was when she took her turn with the rest, getting her fingernails clipped, getting a little sticker on her hand for being good, and of course my weekly hug.

I loved that little girl and she loved me. But our warm relationship could never have existed until she learned to control her own behavior, overcome her fears and be respectful. She would not have done so if I had let her get away with her tantrums and kicking. To have rewarded her negative behavior would not have resulted in our close relationship; it would have prevented it. Instead, she loved me, she loved coming to the nursery and her parents remained active in the Church.

Then I got a phone call. Tonya had run out into the street in front of her house and been struck by a passing car. Her parents asked me to speak at her funeral.

In Conclusion

As you can imagine, some of what you just read about punishment and consequences is equivalent to blasphemy to many psychology professors. I know because I listened to plenty of them on my road to a masters degree in educational psychology. Some of those professors didn't like their doctoral doctrine being questioned by a young upstart from Idaho with only a bachelor's degree in industrial arts.

I believe the Lord knew what he was talking about when he said, "Whom I love I also chasten" (D&C 95:1). Rather than showing that punishment destroys relationships, the scriptures seem to indicate that it can be the very means by which loving relationships are attained.

> My son, despise not thou the chastening of the Lord, nor faint when thou are rebuked of him: For whom the Lord loveth he chasteneth, and scourgeth every son whom he receiveth. . . . No chastening for the present seemeth to be joyous, but grievous: nevertheless *afterward it yieldeth the peaceable fruit of righteousness* unto them which are exercised thereby. [Hebrews 12:5–6, 11; emphasis added]

The Savior's statement, "by their fruits ye shall know them" (Matthew 7:20) applies to principles, doctrines, and philosophies as well as to people. Therefore, as evidence of the effectiveness of the principles of accountability, I present all the children raised under it's influence, and a good balance between love and law.

I also invite those who preach the permissive doctrine of *un*accountability to show us the fruits of *their* teachings. Is the world a better place since permissiveness has become the norm in our homes? For half a century we have done what they have told us to do with our children: fed them, loved them, and left them alone to do as they please. We have blamed everyone and everything else to excuse their actions. Now that the data on every kind of degenerate behavior is coming in, it is clear that the experiment with unaccountability is failing miserably. The problem is, that the preachers of irresponsible doctrine will not accept responsibility for the consequences of their own permissive program.

I invite Church members who believe in the doctrine of unaccountability to do an honest comparison between children of parents who hold them accountable and children of parents who do not. Observe the parenting styles of those with honorable and responsible children, and then compare it to how rebellious and disobedient children were raised. If it is by their fruits that we shall know them, then it is certainly fair to compare the results of different parenting styles. There are exceptions of course, but the consistency in even a casual comparison will speak for itself.

It is impossible to explain in detail how to implement all these principles in every situation, but every one will always involve the principles of agency: multiple options, different consequences and knowledge of the consequences. There are many kinds of consequences to understand. Natural and imposed, positive and negative, immediate and ultimate, temporal and spiritual, known and unknown are just a few. "O be wise; what can I say more?" (Jacob 6:12). *Children taught by the wise use of the principles of agency will eventually learn that decisions should be made based on the appeal of the ultimate outcome, not on the appeal of the immediate choice.*

My only hope is that these principles will bless your life as they have blessed mine. May they also bless the lives of your children as well as those you teach and influence. I also hope that someday,

Chapter 12 — "War" Stories

somehow, this book finds it's way to southern England into the hands of a certain woman whose name I never knew. Unless she reads this, she may never know the effect her question has had on my life. To that young girl who long ago asked me that fateful question, I'd very much like to thank you.

Scripture Index

OLD TESTAMENT

Genesis
3:7–8	56
3:22	66
19:4–9	86

Leviticus
11:44–45	101

Numbers
14:4	45

1 Samuel
17:8	5

1 Kings
12:1–19	45

Job
38:7	40, 43

Isaiah
10:15	49
14:12–13	44
28:10	xiv
29:21	96
48:22	88

NEW TESTAMENT

Matthew
5–7	64
5:48	59
7:14	23
7:18	62
7:20	97, 139

Matthew (cont.)
8:28–29	55
18:7	65
23:23–24	97
23:28	96

Mark
1:23–26	55
5:1–5	55
5:1–15	63
5:15	63
9:17–22	55

Luke
12:42	27
14:27	75
15:3–7	129
15:8–10	129
15:20	130
15:13	129
16:1–2	27

John
3:16	105
3:19	57
3:20	57
5:39	102
6:5–13	93
6:26 (JST)	93
6:66	93
7:7	59

14:15	105	10:23	14, 17
John (cont.)		**2 Nephi** (cont.)	
14:21	105	25:23	59
Galatians		26:27	10
6:7	30	28:3–4	56
2 Thessalonians		28:5	57
2:12	58	28:7	57
3:10	93	28:7–8	74
Hebrews		28:8	58, 75
12:5–6, 11	139	28:9	58
1 Peter		28:20	59
3:15	xiii	28:21	59
Revelation		28:22	58
5:1–4	42	**Jacob**	
5:1–14	65	6:12	140
5:3–5	41	7:4	70, 83
5:5–9	43	**Mosiah**	
5:11–13	43	2:16–23	93
12:4	23, 40, 70, 76	2:21	59
12:10	45, 70	3:11	31
22:16	40	3:19	45
		4:9	49
		4:14–15	107

BOOK OF MORMON

1 Nephi		4:30	xiv
4:1	49	5:8	18
11:21–23	105	10:12–13	85
11:25	105	29:25	83
15:34	49	29:26	85
19:23	102	**Alma**	
2 Nephi		11:21	70
2:4	10	12:14	xiv
2:11	3, 21	14:8–10	73
2:26–27	18	15:15	73
2:29	35	30:10–11	11
4:34	98	30:10, 18	83
9:7–9	19	30:17–18	85
9:28	74	30:18	12, 88, 98, 99
9:48	59	30:24	11

30:28	12	14:30	30
Alma (cont.)		**3 Nephi**	
30:42, 53	70	1:29	83
30:47	83	3:5	85
30:53	83	3:6–10	85
30:9–11	71	3:7	86
31:9, 16	72	3:19	85, 87
31:15–17	72	6:27–28	81
40:13	122	**Mormon**	
41:10	35, 72, 108, 123	2:13	121
42:1	21	**Ether**	
42:13	32, 72	8:2	83
42:16	121	8:16	81, 82
42:17	21, 107	8:17	79, 84
42:22	106	8:20–25	91
42:24–25	58	8:22	88
42:25	76, 107	8:25	82
42:27	15	9:11	92
42:8, 16	123	12:27	113
43:9	80	**Moroni**	
47:18	86	7:6–10	64
54:17	85	7:16–18	33
61:4	83	10:32	60
Helaman		**DOCTRINE & COVENANTS**	
2:1–5	79		
2:5	83	1:16	35
4:22	84	1:31	46, 56, 107, 108
4:22–24	84	1:31, 16	74
5:2	86	6:9	59
5:2–3	84	9:8	xiv
5:10–11	73	19:15	109
6:21	84	29:35	26
6:26	83	29:36	23, 44, 46, 49, 76
6:27	45	29:47	105
6:38	82, 85, 87, 99	29:47–50	31
6:39	79, 80, 86, 99	42:32	27
13:27	52	42:88–93	107
13:38	74, 88	45:3–5	50

D&C		
50:10	xiv, 101	
D&C (cont.)		
57:6	29, 30	
58:30	35, 109	
58:30–32	71, 77	
64:12–13	107	
64:18	29	
64:29	28	
64:34	63	
70:3–4, 9–11	28	
72:3	77	
72:31	28	
76:25	50, 66	
76:25–26	39	
76:26	40	
76:28	44	
76:29	vii	
77:6	42	
84:113	28	
88:6–7	40	
88:34–38	105	
88:36–38	10	
88:118	xiv	
93:30	62	
93:31	31	
93:36	40	
95:1	139	
98:8	10	
101:78	31	
104:11–13, 17	30	
105:5	71	
122:7	65	
130:20–21	20, 106	
132:11	9	
132:11–12	105	
132:20–22	101	
132:20–23	71	
132:22	23	

PEARL OF GREAT PRICE

Moses

3:16–17	16
3:17	32
4:1	40, 41, 44, 45, 47, 50, 51, 61, 69, 70
4:1, 3	48
4:1–2	47
4:2	48
4:3	viii, 21, 23, 25, 36, 46, 49, 50, 106
4:6	50
4:11	66
4:30	110, 113
5:10–11	65
5:11	65
5:24	76
5:31	88
6:55	104
7:32	32

Abraham

3:26	65
3:28	51

Index

Abuse:
    fear of keeps parents from punishing, 108
    must be avoided, 108
    only extreme punishment is, 108
    is not the most common problem, 108

Accountability:
    is agency, 25, 29
    is stewardship, 27, 76
    in eternity, 28
    requires knowledge, 31
    is more than freedom, 31–32
    Adam and Eve had, in the garden, 32
    man's desire to avoid, 35
    redeeming all mankind attacks, 46
    attempts to avoid, 56;
    found in the pure doctrine of Christ, 60, 75
    destroyed by saving in sin, 68
    Alma upheld, 71
    people of Ammonihah rejected, 73
    Anti-Christ doctrine based on, 74
    efforts to reduce, 74–75
    Gadiantons sought to avoid, 82–83
    Gadiantons destroyed, by degrees, 86
    desire to escape, is reason for Nephite fall, 87
    people who accept, are not easily deceived, 87
    modern Gadiantons also avoid, 91
    compassion should not sacrifice, 93
    mutual, between people and government, 94
    of children to parents before age eight, 105
    prodigal sons were not taught, 111
    teaching children, helps them to be responsible, 112
    avoiding, was Satan's plan, 114
    outside influences rarely overcome well taught, 114–115
    practiced by the Murphy's, 118–120

Act(s):
    for yourselves, explanation of, 17–18, 30, 31
    everyone to be saved regardless of, 69

Adam:
    free to partake of tree, 16
    had stewardship in the garden, 32
    attempt to hide shame, 56
    statement from, about transgression, 65
    children of, tasted bitter to prize the good, 104

Adultery:
   Korihor's agenda concerning, 11–13, 83, 98

Agency:
   every decision is the exercise of, xiv
   is central to the plan, xiv–xv, 33
   not the same as choice or freedom, 1
   requires knowledge of results, 3, 33
   is not without penalty, 15–16
   misunderstanding causes trouble, 23
   principles of, fundamental to entire plan, 24
   false definition of, 23–24
   the three requirements of, 25, 33, 106
   definition of, 25, 29
   is stewardship and accountability, 25, 29, 31–32
   is not "free agency," 34
   destroyed by eliminating any one requirement, 36, 106
   J. R. Clark says two ways to destroy it, 68,
   war on, continued by Gadiantons, 99
   present when God gives commandments, 106
   only ones understanding of can be destroyed, 109
   teaching, helps in raising responsible children, 112
   using to our advantage by making right choices, 123

Agent(s):
   is a steward, 25–26
   the word in the D&C, 28
   a bishop is an, 28
   is appointed to a business, 28
   meaning of, unto themselves, 30

Agentship:
   is agency, 26

Alma:
   enforced divine laws, 71

Ammonihah:
   people of, abandoned accountability, 73

Amulek:
   said Christ saves from not in sin, 73

Atonement:
   brings spiritual freedom, 18–19
   results limited without, 20
   added a reward, 20
   understood better through agency, 24
   Messiah must fulfill demands of, 42

Benson, Ezra Taft:
   said war in heaven was like a political struggle, 91
   said saints should support freedom, 92
   encourages self help not government support, 94

Bible:
   mentions steward not agent, 25

Bishop:
   is an agent, 28

Blame:
   useful tool in raising an irresponsible child, 110
   do not, when raising responsible children, 113

Book:
   that no man could open, 42
   represents the mission of the Messiah, 42
   Christ prevailed to open, 42–43

Building:
burning, example of, 7

Cannon, George Q.:
said Satan's plan was to save everyone regardless of choices, 69

Children:
act with limited accountability, 31
do come with a manual, 102
generations of influenced by true principles, 102
targeted by Satan, 103
why they think life is like University of Freedom, 103
from permissive homes struggle to use agency wisely, 104
respond to love early 105
accountable to parents before age eight, 105

Choice(s):
requires two options, 2, 5, 7
definition of, 5, 6
don't have to be opposite, 6, 15
different from freedom, 6
not having, 7
with or without penalty, 11–13
includes freedom to lose, 21
does not require knowledge, 31
not different if results are the same, 67, 72
not limited in Satan's plan, 69
different results of, will teach, 114
Murphy's made children accountable for, 118–120

Christ:
known as the morning star, 40
the only one qualified, 41–42
account of choosing as Messiah, 41–43
did not propose a plan, 48
pleads to Father in our behalf, 50
fed the 5,000, only once, 93
his compassion did not sacrifice accountability, 93

Clark, J. Reuben
questioned the force plan, 62–63
says there is more than one way to destroy agency, 68

Coins:
used in object lesson, 1–2

Compassion:
misguided when accountability is sacrificed, 93
not, when help is not needed, 93

Compulsion:
spiritual freedom is without, 14–16
is one way to destroy agency, 68

Condemnation:
agency makes possible, 31
none without knowledge, 31

Consequences:
decisions made without regard to, 35
need to teach, of sin, 59
different, makes choices different, 67
natural, still applied in Satan's plan, 71
of believing in no consequences, 72
Darwinism decreases concern for, 73–74
anti-Christs and Gadiantons seek to avoid, 83
limiting limits freedom, 88–89
always given when God gives commandments, 106
delivery of is often missing, 106
irresponsible children produced by not facing, 109–111

hard, of life can teach children
    responsibility, 111
different, for different behavior,
    112
should be explained to raise
    responsible children, 112
promised, must be delivered to
    raise responsible children, 112,
    127–128
of failure are good learning
    experiences, 114
unpleasant, need not damage
    relationships, 117–118
immediate and ultimate, 124
will teach what parents do not, 127
Corianton:
    sought condition without penalty,
    21
Couch:
    story of the old, 121–122
    how children sat on to solve their
    problems, 121–122
Darwin:
    explanation of popularity of theory,
    73–74
Dependence:
    opposite to independence, 94
    creating, upon parents raises
    irresponsible children, 109
Devil:
    meaning of, 45
    if none, then no fear of
    consequences, 58
Distraction:
    used by Gadiantons, 99
    use, to raise irresponsible children,
    109
    avoid, to raise responsible children,
    112

Emotions:
    power of negative, 51
    motivated the rebellion, 51, 55
Family:
    a target of Gadiantons, 95
    best defense against war on agency,
    99
    why Satan attacks, 99
    many unknowingly practice Satan's
    plan, 100
Father, Heavenly:
    chose Jesus as the Messiah, 41–42
    on the throne, 42
    outlined the plan, 45
    Jesus supported his plan, 48
    all powerful, 49–50
    the ultimate judge of man, 49–50
    omniscient, 51
    accused by Satan, 70–71
    exercised agency to end war in
    heaven, 76
    preserve agency like, to raise
    responsible children, 112
Flattery:
    anti-Christs and Satan use, 70, 83
    used by Gadiantons to corrupt
    laws, 83–84
    of fair promises, 84
Forbidden fruit:
    free to partake of, 16–17
Force College:
    description of, 52
    has little appeal, 54–55
    is not like Satan's plan, 55–56
    loss of freedom obvious in, 60
    parents attempt to avoid, 107
Force plan:
    not scriptural, xi–xiv, 55–56, 61

belief in causes misunderstandings, 15
only one possibility, 36
explanation of possible source, 48–49
doesn't stir up emotions, 51
compared to Force College, 52–55
evil not a choice in, 61
is not logical for three reasons, 62–64
questioned by J. Reuben Clark, 62–63
could not produce righteousness, 62–64
flaws too obvious, 64–65
not clever or enticing, 66
is compulsion of the mind, 68
misunderstood by parents, 107, 126

Free:
compared to freedom, 11
politically, is choice without penalty, 16–17
spiritually, is choice without compulsion, 16–17, 34
without agency, 34

Freedom plan:
brilliance and deception of, 66
destroys freedom, 67
the second possibility for Satan's plan, 68
offered freedom from failure and punishment, 71
popularity of, 72–73, 88–89
philosophies of men embrace, 73
why it appeals to religious also, 73
used by Gadiantons, 77–80, 83
encourages dependence, 94
Satan's favorite strategy, 99, 103
practiced in many LDS homes, 100
why children think life is like, 103
offers love without law, 104

Freedom:
requires different results, 2–4, 8, 15, 19
different from choice, 6–8, 21
requires law, 9
definitions of, 3, 8, 9, 14, 67–68, 96
not without cost, 10–11
includes penalty, 14–19, 21
spiritual, is choice without compulsion, 14–17
political, is choice without penalty, 14–15
spiritual, three characteristics of, 18
comes because of atonement, 18–20
includes freedom to lose, 21
meaning has been twisted, 35
guaranteed government programs subversive to, 92
must be guarded continually, 94
dependence limits, 94
God creates, by giving us option to fail, 106

Gadiantons:
used flattery on Nephites, 51, 83
used Satan's plan, 77, 82–83, 99
took the Nephite Government, 77
were the highest level of secret combination, 81
made oaths with each other, 81
methods of getting elected, 82, 83–85, 98–99
made secrecy the highest priority, 82
used seduction, 82
taught the freedom plan, 83
corrupted Nephite laws, 83–84

brotherhood promised protection,
    84–85
accused their enemies, 85
took power the Nephites gave
    them, 85–87
how they got what they wanted
    from the Nephites, 86–87
modern, do the same things, 91
use money to become popular, 91
prefer hand out to hand up, 93
today's, use political correctness,
    95–96
bleed the system of its economy, 99

Gilbert, Sidney:
appointed as an agent and told to
    return to his agency, 29

Goliath:
example using, 5

Government:
Nephite, taken over by
    Gadiantons, 77, 79
support from is control from, 92–93
should have mutual accountability
    with people, 94
not all Gadiantons are in, 95
political correctness of Gadiantons
    in, 97

Grace:
saved by, 20, 59–60
perfected by, 60
doctrine of, alone reduces
    accountability, 75
doctrine of, alone close to Satan's
    plan, 75

Happiness:
wickedness never was, 35, 72, 108
unaccountability is contrary to, 35
seeking, in doing iniquity, 74, 88

some believe entertainment is the
    key to, 111
doing what is right is the key to,
    114, 123
punishment is opposite to the plan
    of, 121
we have responsibility for our own,
    121, 122
plan of, called plan of salvation,
    123
making choices that bring, 123

Hollywood:
Gadiantons among, 95
agenda is in their scripts, 97
advertises the doctrine of Korihor,
    97

Independence:
opposite to dependence, 94

Injustice:
accountability without knowledge
    violates, 32
Satan accused Father of, 71

Irresponsible:
how to raise an, child 109–111
children sometimes become,
    regardless of best efforts, 114
parents are reason why some
    children are, 126

John (the Revelator):
account of the book no man could
    open, 42
saw rejoicing when Christ was
    chosen, 43
defines Devil, 45

Justice:
requires knowledge before
    accountability, 32

Knowledge:
    of results, required for agency, 3
    is required for accountability, 30–31
    is the light of Christ, 33
    of good and evil deprived in force plan, 65–66

Korihor:
    example using, 11
    had characteristics like Satan, 70
    used seduction, 83
    was taught by Satan, 83

Lamanites:
    methods of attempts on Nephite government, 79

Law School:
    description of, 53
    represents Father's plan, 55

Law(s):
    required for freedom, 9–10
    designate, but do not restrict, 10
    attach consequences to decisions, 10
    Korihors objection to, 11–13
    must include penalty, 23
    Gadiantons corrupt Nephite, 82–83
    how divine, are corrupted, 84, 99
    without love is like Satan's plan 106
    necessity of, and love 106–107
    lack of is the problem, 106–107
    are what the prodigal son didn't like, 130

Lee, Harold B.:
    used scriptures to answer questions, xiii

Love:
    without law is Satan's plan, 104, 106–107
    God uses, and law, 105
    definition of, 105
    lack of, is not the problem, 105
    disobedience not conducive to, 108
    used to justify permissiveness, 111
    justifies not protecting children from consequences, 114
    is the reason why the Prodigal son came home, 130

Lucifer:
    a son of the morning, 40
    meaning of, 40
    status of before his fall, 39–40
    wanted to be the Messiah, 41, 45, 61, 65
    envied Christ, 44
    desired power, 44–45
    motivated by negative emotions, 51
    changed definition of freedom, 68–69
    used a kind of political correctness, 96

McConkie, Bruce R.:
    defines agency, 33
    paraphrased Satan's plan, 41
    calls "two plans" heresy, 48

Mercy:
    unconditional, is Satan's plan, 72

Messiah:
    mission of, represented by the book, 42
    Lucifer wanted to be, 41, 45, 61
    we need one to be redeemed, 61–62

Money:
   used by Gadiantons to become popular, 91

Moral agency:
   is moral accountability, 31
   an alternative to "free agency," 34

Murphy's:
   story of responsible children of, 117–120

Nephites:
   tried to preserve their freedom, 79–80
   supported the Gadiantons, 82, 84–86
   motives for supporting Gadiantons, 82
   seduced by fair promises, 84
   gave power to Gadiantons, 84–86
   laws of became corrupt, 83–84
   united with Gadiantons, 84–86
   rejected Gadiantons when righteous, 85
   why they destroyed themselves, 88

Neuenschwander, Dennis B.:
   defines agency, 33
   says war in heaven was a battle over responsibility, 36

Oaks, Dallen H.:
   said unconditional salvation is Satan's plan, 72

Object lesson:
   of two coins, 1–4, 6, 15, 21, 67

Opposition:
   requires different results, 21
   agency requires, 33
   some still applied in Satan's plan, 71

Parent(s):
   unknowingly practice Satan's plan, 100, 103, 107
   God is the perfect, 101
   stewardships as, most important, 101
   true principles of, 102
   scriptures are the source of skills of, 102
   applying principles of appropriately, 102
   who practice love without law destroy relationships, 106–108
   how they can raise an irresponsible child, 109–111
   distrusted by irresponsible children, 110
   are trusted by responsible children, 113
   prophets know more than professors about being, 111, 114

Penalty:
   required for agency, 14, 21
   false notions about threats of, 15
   required for spiritual freedom, 19, 21
   Corianton sought to escape, 21
   Satan's plan sought to eliminate, 71, 117
   home becomes a University of Freedom without, 107
   elimination of, helps produce an irresponsible child, 109–111
   need not destroy relationships, 117–118
   can be effective with love, 117–118

Pennies:
   object lesson using, 1–4, 5, 21

example of cashier using, 6–7
if representing hell, 20, 32, 67
compared to atonement, 20
if representing heaven, 32, 68

Perdition:
meaning of, 40

Permissive parents:
how they raise irresponsible children, 102–104
in direct conflict with learning from experience, 104
promote Satan's plan, 104, 107
children of, have trouble accepting responsibility, 107
become, out of fear to abuse, 108

Plan, Satan's:
diabolical brilliance of, 21, 66
explanation of source of force plan, 48–49
enticement of, 51
did not limit choices, 69–70
made no demands on us, 70
arguments for, 71
has not changed, 76
popular among the Nephites, 88–89
encourages dependence on Satan, 94
helpful in raising irresponsible children, 109–111
avoiding accountability was, 114

Political correctness:
a flattering new vocabulary called, 95–96
Lucifer used a kind of, 96
the purpose of, 97–98
use of, by Hollywood, Government and schools, 97
flattery of, provides cloak of hypocritical righteousness, 97–98

Power to choose:
not having, 6–7

Punishment:
being acted upon by, 18–19
essential to agency, 106–107
God uses on his children, 106
disuse of is the most common problem, 108
do not use to raise an irresponsible child, 109–111
false beliefs about, 110–111
use appropriate, when necessary, 112
deliver promised, to develop trust, 113
trauma from appropriate, will not damage relationship, 114
we must use, appropriately, 117
must be opposite to happiness, 121

Question(s):
about Satan's force plan, viii
answered by H. B. Lee, xiii

Rebellion:
of Satan explained, 49–50
Satans, was against God and Christ, 50
an attempt to persuade God to forfeit power, 50
was illogical, 51
motivated by negative emotions, 51
was a war fought on two fronts, 71
why many children practice, 99–100
children in, have not suffered enough, 104

raising children responsibly will usually avoid, 114
children are often trained in, 120
can justly result in being cast out, 129
of a young man told to leave home, 130

Redeem(ed):
being, from fall results in freedom, 19–20
offer of being, precludes force plan, 61–62, 65
joy of being, known by Adam & Eve, 65
offer to, without requirements, 68–69

Relationship(s):
between choice, freedom and agency, 1
between stewardship and accountability, 27–28
between beliefs and behavior, 56–57
between Gadiantons and the people, 84–87
between dependence and independence, 94
with our children changed by scriptures, 102
loving, require law and love, 105
no loving, in home with law without love, 106
loving, disobedience not conducive to, 108
abuse destroys, 108
losing trust damages, 110
false belief that punishment will always damage, 111, 117–118
trust establishes vital, 113
punishment need not damage, 114–118
risk to, is minimal if love is present, 117–118

Religion:
a target of Gadiantons, 95

Requirements of agency:
three, 1–4

Responsibility:
is agency, 25, 29
war in heaven was a battle over, 36
is someone else's, to some children, 107
not usually learned by children of permissive parenting, 110–111
taught to children by the Murphy's, 118–120
learned by children whose parents teach, 120
for happiness is upon the individual, 122
we sometimes assume to much of others, 121
to attempt to retrieve lost coin and sheep, 129

Righteousness:
compulsory, is not real, 62–63
force plan could not produce, 62–63

Satan:
disguises his plan, 23
plan of, exposed, 24
author of doctrine of unaccountability, 36
doesn't want exposure, 37
was "in authority," 40
what sparked his rebellion, 41

wanted to be the Messiah, 41,
    44–45
desired power, 44–45
offered an alternative plan, 47
rebellion was against God and
    Christ, 50
motivated by negative emotions, 51
stirs up people to anger, 59
lulls people to hell, 59
the accuser of our brethren, 70
characteristics of, 70
why he attacks the family, 95, 99
uses permissive parents to promote
    his plan, 103
force was not his plan, 111
wanted to reward negative
    behavior, 120
Scriptures:
force plan not found in, xii, 48,
    55–56
source of truth, xiv
tell us of war in heaven, 23
words for freedom in, 31
"free agency" not found in, 34
never state Jesus offered a plan, 47
support University of Freedom as
    Satan's plan, 56–59
attempts to avoid accountability in,
    56
say results are limited in Satan's
    plan, 69–70
teach us of our obligations to poor,
    93
are the source of parenting skills
    and principles, 102
teach us how God teaches his
    children, 102
Secret combinations:
definition of, 81

survived under freedom plan, 85,
    88
Sherem:
had characteristics like Satan, 70
Smith, Joseph:
said freedoms would be bartered
    away, 80
Spanking:
a consequence used to teach
    happiness, 125
Steward(s):
is an agent, 25–26
definition of, 27
in modern scripture, 27
Stewardship:
is agency, 26, 76
is agentship, 26
definition of, 27
is accountability, 27
Adam and Eve had, in the garden,
    32
destroyed by saving in sin, 68–69

Taylor, John:
quotes Joseph Smith on bartering
    freedom, 80
Traditions:
popular but not scriptural, xii
about two plans, 47–48
about the force plan, 48
about the source of the force plan,
    48
Tree of knowledge of good and evil:
Adam free to partake of, 16–17
Trust:
must be avoided to raise an
    irresponsible child, 110
essential in raising responsible
    children, 113
how to develop, 113

Two plans:
  illogical and not scriptural, xii

University of Freedom:
  description of, 52–53
  compared to Force College, 52–56
  is like Satan's plan, 56
  offers choice but no freedom, 60
  why children think life is like, 103
  Satan and permissive parents promote, 103–104, 107

War in Heaven:
  was a battle over responsibility, 36
  force plan was only one possibility, 36
  Satan doesn't want plan concerning exposed, 37
  was not an attempt to compel God, 49
  was over stewardship and accountability, 76
  was like a political struggle, 91
  Lucifer used a kind of political correctness in, 96
  has come to earth, 98–99, 117
  story of, helps parents, 129

Zeezrom:
  had characteristics like Satan, 70
  Amulek taught, in Ammonihah, 73

Zoramites:
  believed in unconditional salvation, 72